For Frank,
with every bestwish
for the future
Frank Z. Pittinger 1
26 · vi · 94

FRANK KEMPE
From an original drawing by Robin Wiggins

THE PLAY'S THE THING

A CRITIC'S HISTORY OF THE THEATRE
IN
NORTH DEVON

Frank Kempe

WESTWELL
DEVON
ISBN 0- 9521413- 3- 7

Westwell Publishing
Friendship
Guineaford
Marwood
Devon
EX31 4EA

The Play's The Thing

A Critic's History of the Theatre in North Devon

Frank Kempe

Typeset, Printed, and Bound by
The Lazarus Press
Devon England EX39 2EA

Cover Design & Artwork Peter Rothwell © 1995

PUBLISHERS' NOTES

We would like to thank North Devon District Council for their help in this venture.

The Staff of the Queen's Theatre has from the start, been most kind and supportive and we thank them for all their encouragement.

We would also like to thank all the people who have loaned photographs – we have not been able to use them all, partly because there were so many and partly because of the technical difficulties of reproduction, but our thanks are, nonetheless, heartfelt.

Our deepest thanks are also due to the North Devon Journal for publishing our requests for photographs, and reminders to Subscribers, and for permission to use photographs. We thank RL Knights of Barnstaple (who took most of the photographs we have used); Baths Photographic; and John Baxter of Ilfracombe for permission to use their photographs; also John Down, Bob Aston, Charlie Lewis and John Molland for help in collecting photographs.

We would also like to thank our subscribers. If we have missed you off the list, we apologise, but, with a publication date to achieve, we could not, with *Time's wingèd chariot hurrying near* telephone everyone FHK mentioned, to remind them that we had written.

Finally and most particularly we wish to thank Mrs Beryl Kempe for all her invaluable help and advice, without which we could not have managed.

To my wife Beryl
who has driven me to
thousands of Theatrical performances.
Having experienced my driving, she
regards this as a major contribution to
the Road safety Campaign.
I also thank her for typing the
manuscript and for deciphering
my rough notes.

Mrs Freda Abraham, Shirwell Cross • Barnstaple
Bob Aston, Atlantic Way • Westward Ho!
William & Susan Atkins, The Quay • Bideford
Phyllis Babb, Exeter Street • Salisbury
Graham Bailey, Newport • Barnstaple
Sheila Bawden, Sticklepath • Barnstaple
Beaford Centre, Beaford • Winkleigh
RH Beattie, Church Lane • Barnstaple
Pamela Beecham, Shoestring Arts • Ilfracombe
Noel Beer , Rayleigh • Essex
Rev. WG Benson, Roundswell • Barnstaple
Henry Blacksell, Chiswick • London
Mr & Mrs AWJ Blake, Fremington • Barnstaple
Carol (Cresswell) Blight, Saunton Park • Braunton
Rick & Charlotte Bond, The Queen's Theatre • Barnstaple
Mr & Mrs Bosworth, Sticklepath • Barnstaple
Roy Boucher Atlantic Way • Westward Ho!
Mrs R Bridle, Woody Bay • Barnstaple
Patrick & Mary Brighten, Playford Mill • Pilton
Jose Burrow, Fairy Cross • Bideford
KJ Burrow, Bucks Cross • Bideford
Louise Cann, Linden Close • Barnstaple
Julie Carder, Elwell Cottage • West Buckland
Andrew Challacombe, Kings Nympton • Umberleigh
Geoffrey Challacombe, Braunton Road • Barnstaple
Roger & Paula Chapple, Chumhill • Bratton Fleming
Brian & Mary Chugg, Sharlands House • Braunton
Douglas J Cock, Heavitree • Exeter
Miss Evelyn Cornell, Dulverton • Somerset
Janet Cotter, Lower Winsham Farm • Braunton
AJ Crighton, Kingsley Avenue • Ilfracombe
Brian Cummings, Kent Gardens • Ealing
Miss Frances Mary Curry, Broadfield Road • Barnstaple
Mike Davey, Sowden Park • Barnstaple
Joan Davies, Old Post Cottage • Mortehoe
Mrs J Dawson, Prixford • Barnstaple
Hilda Dix, Barnstaple • *3 copies*
John Down, High Bickington • *2 Copies*
Dulverton Players, Dulverton • Somerset
John & Jane Dunsdon, Rose-in-the-Grove • Eckworthy
Tony Evans, Willow Cottage • Braunton
Angela Ford, Moorcroft • Bovey Tracey
Terry Ford, Martin Road • Barnstaple
Major JP Foulds, Bull Hill • Pilton
G Ivor Gammon, North Morte Road • Mortehoe
Edward Gaskell & Rebecca Renouf, Riverbank Cottages • Bideford
Miss Natalie Gaskell, Victoria Gardens • Bideford
Stuart Gaydon, Priory Gardens • Barnstaple
Mr P Godfrey, Portland Street • Barnstaple
Su Scott Goldstone, Broad Park Avenue • Ilfracombe
Mr & Mrs G Green, Pinhoe • Exeter
John M Gregory, Bickington • Barnstaple
Sheila M Gregory, Bickington • Barnstaple
Rosemary Hart, Brushford • Dulverton
Jim Hawkins, Taddiport • West Buckland
Ian Henderson-Begg Chittlehampton • Umberleigh
John & Melanie Hornby, Barbican Terrace • Barnstaple

Everard Howard, Chittlehampton • Umberleigh
Chris Jackson, Elmsleigh • Combe Martin
Julia Jenkins, Fremington • Barnstaple
Harold Jester, Brislington • Bristol
Peter Jewell, Park Lane • Barnstaple
Miss Minnie Joint, Barum Court • Barnstaple
Chris & Gill Jones, Topsham • Exeter
Keith Jones, Brannams Court • Barnstaple
Gordon Kennon Ashleigh Road • Barnstaple
Beryl Kempe, Alma Place • Barnstaple
John Lane, Beaford • Winkleigh
Lazarus Press (Edward Gaskell) Grenville Street • Bideford
Daphne & Bob Lock, Bickleigh • Ilfracombe
Denis Loosemoore, Ashford • Barnstaple
Chris & Sandra Lovering, Old Sticklepath Hill • Barnstaple
Mr D McCallam, Shackhayes • Combe Martin
Lynda McLaughlin, David Close • Braunton   2 copies
John Marks, Shute Lane • Combe Martin
John Molland, Ceramic Terrace • Barnstaple
Peter & Julie Moore, Castle Hill Terrace • Ilfracombe
North Devon Journal(Colin Davison) High Street • Barnstaple
Glyn Parsley, Pinhoe • Exeter
Sally Petley, Waikenae • New Zealand
Alan & Mary Phillips, Crofts Lea Park • Ilfracombe
Graham Poat, Dulverton • Somerset
David Pote & Maureen Sharpe, Cambridge Grove • Ilfracombe
Andre Potier, Silver Street • Barnstaple
Charles & Betty Price, St Brannocks Place • Ilfracombe
Richard Quick, Fleet Road • Hampstead
Keith Rattray, Exeter • Devon
Les & Doreen Reading, Ilfracombe • Devon
Roger & Chris Reeve, Church Street • Braunton
O C Riedel, Ashford • Barnstaple
PJ Roberts, Oakland Park South • Barnstaple
Miss EJ Robins, Summerland Street • Barnstaple
Molly Rose, Stowe Barton • Kilkhampton
Peter Rothwell (Westwell Publishing) Goosewell • Berrynarbour   2 Copies
Jillian Rowe, Catcott • Bridgewater
Marion Scotting, Tawstock • Barnstaple
Sarah Small, Loxhore • Barnstaple
Don Smy, Fremington • Barnstaple
Joan E Spear, Pilton • Barnstaple
Carol & Gill Taylor, Exwick • Exeter
Bob Terrell, Newton Tracey • Barnstaple
Rose Todd, Higher Park Road • Braunton
June Tollafield, Upper Gorwell House • Barnstaple
Katie Tucker, Rolle Street • Barnstaple
Mark Turvey, Stapleton Road • London
Jane (Bryan) Vandenbrouk, Horwood • Newton Tracey
Barbara Wearne, The Quay • Instow
Ann Westcott (Westwell Publishing) Guineaford • Marwood   2 Copies
Richard Wheeler, New Road • Instow
John Willey, The Small House • Heanton
Florence Williams, Poole • Dorset
Mr & Mrs JC Williams, Newton Tracey • Barnstaple
Mrs J Wright, Fort Hill • Barnstaple

LIST OF ILLUSTRATIONS

Frontispiece :   Line Drawing of the author   Page i

CONTENTS

Preface

So far as I know, this is the first history of North Devon theatre to be published in book form. I was asked to undertake the writing, presumably because I have been a theatre critic operating in the area through five decades.

These duties have involved me in producing about 6,000 reviews of productions ranging from those of the Royal Shakespeare Company to the efforts of sundry Barnstaple and Ilfracombe Schools of Dance.

Local historians – notably W F Gardiner, Sydney Harper and Lois Lamplugh – have included references to theatre in their publications. Like an upstart crow, beautified by the feathers of others, I have borrowed on these. But I have concentrated particularly on the development of North Devon theatre during the past fifty years.

This has been a period of prolific expansion. In 1939, when I began reviewing, there were about eight productions a year in the area, mostly musicals and by amateurs. In 1989, when I made my last count, there were nearly 100, about half by professional groups.

Moreover, the quality of the plays undertaken has steadily improved. The classics are now well represented, as are modern plays dealing with social issues. The latter have replaced the spate of light comedies, previously conspicuous in the dramatic fare.

My own enthusiasm for the theatre may have been inherited from my paternal grandfather, who was headmaster of a school in South Devon. It was certainly augmented by the experience of my early teens.

As a schoolboy I spent much of the summer break, between spring and autumn terms, in London. This enabled me to see in action the likes of John Gielgud, Ralph Richardson, Ivor Novello, Sybil Thorndike, Peggy Ashcroft and Max Miller. At their various levels they were experiences that I shall never forget.

The Press in North Devon has paid increasing and discerning

interest to theatre during the past half-century. I am personally grateful to the *North Devon Journal, The Stage* (the newspaper of the acting profession), *The Western Morning News*, and more recently *The North Devon Advertiser* for providing me with pulpits from which to pontificate.

My appointment as deputy editor of the *Journal* with responsibility for editorial layout, gave me an opportunity to assign at least one page of each issue to news and views on theatre and other artistic events.

Critics invariably receive more hostile criticism than they deliver, to which the 'letters' column in the *Journal* will testify. On one occasion, I even had a sermon preached against me, following a particularly favourable notice of a production of Sartre's *The Respectable Prostitute* at Ilfracombe. On the following Sunday an evangelical vicar denounced in no uncertain manner the action of 'a respectable newspaper' (the *Journal*) in allowing its critic to recommend such a play.

In fact, the preacher had obviously not taken my advice to visit the production. It involved the Colour Bar, still rampant in America at that time, rather than the oldest profession. But critics should be the last persons to resent criticism, however unfairly based, of themselves.

I have served on a variety of organisations involved with the arts, these including the advisory committees of *the North Devon College, the Orchard Theatre, Barnstaple Playgoers' Circle*, and *the North Devon Drama Federation*, of which I was chairman.

When I retired as deputy editor of the *Journal* in 1984, I received 200 letters and cards of congratulations, mostly from those whose work I had reviewed. I would like to think of them as goodwill gestures rather than as being sent in the spirit of relief. In fact, I continued to master-mind the *Journal* arts coverage until 1992. It is now directed by my former collaborator, an able young journalist, Sarah Small.

1

Hobby-Horse to Shakespeare

There is little evidence to show how theatre as we know it came to North Devon. Presumably, it was brought by bands of strolling players sometime during the 14th and 15th centuries. They would probably have come from the larger cities, travelling the roads with horse and cart on what would now be termed provincial tours.

Their repertoire might have included crude comedies and possibly plays on religious themes. Their activities were somewhat encouraged, albeit from a distance, by the Roman Catholic Church.

The old pre-Christian beliefs of Pagan worship were still flourishing in the remote country districts. Even today what was once a Pagan revel is still celebrated annually at Combe Martin. Although updated to embrace a legend of the Jacobean era, it is almost certainly a relic of an ancient fertility rite. Spread over three days in the season of Ascension, it ranks as a form of street theatre, being known as the Hunting of the Earl of Rone. The Irish earl was a strong opponent of English intervention in Ireland and in this capacity he incurred the wrath of the English government; the legend grew that when he fled from Ireland, with English militia in hot pursuit, he was shipwrecked in the Bristol Channel and made his landing on Combe Martin beach.

Each Whitsun he is hunted, captured, and led through the streets, seated back to front on a donkey. At intervals he is dismounted and shot by an escort of Grenadiers. At sundown his effigy is thrown into the sea.

The hobby-horse revel was banned during the 1830s, following representations by a local Nonconformist minister, who alleged that it created drunkenness and debauchery. It was revived by local folk

1

enthusiasts during the 1970s and is now established as a regular event. Whether the reputation of the proceedings for stimulating licentious behaviour has been maintained is a matter of conjecture.

The story commemorated is only marginally related to fact. Tyrone did flee Ireland, but he was never shipwrecked and made a safe landing on the Continent, where he was fêted by the Pope. But the celebration of his liquidation is one of the oldest-established theatrical events that North Devon enjoys. It is also one in which the involvement of local inhabitants has been retained. Turning it into a tourist attraction, to benefit Combe Martin's hotel industry, is a development that the revivalists have been keen to avoid.

Christmas in North Devon has lately been commemorated not only with pantomimes but with a mummer's play. 'St George and the Turkish Knight' is usually presented not in playhouses but in selected local pubs. It is almost certainly a survival of the Old Religion, a fertility rite which welcomed the arrival of Spring. The local tour usually covers an area from Yarde Down to Lee Bay.

St George, the hero of the story, is not necessarily the patron saint of England, notorious among Animal Rights activists for his prowess in killing dragons. The plot involves him in mortal combat, first with the Bold Slasher and then with the Turk of the title. But when protagonists are killed they are restored miraculously to life.

The mummers arrive unheralded as far as customers are concerned and hammer a demand for entrance on the pub door.

The humour is broad and the characters are colourful. They include Father Christmas, a mercenary Quack Doctor and Beelzebub, who usually passes round the hat. Father Christmas, traditionally the bagman, is a relatively recent addition, having been introduced in medieval times. He is represented as a somewhat tetchy old man, much removed from the jolly Santa Claus who is beloved by departmental stores.

The story is presented in rhyming couplets, originally handed down from one generation to the next by word of mouth.

The enactment was once a regular feature of country life in Britain. Now it exists in only a few areas, of which North Devon is one.

The nomadic mummers of Medieval days found themselves as welcome in North Devon as New Age travellers would be today.

Actors were classed socially with vagabonds and rogues. There was at least one good practical reason for this hostility. Visitors from 'foreign parts' were generally discouraged because it was feared that they might bring with them the infection of the Black Death, which had decimated the population in other parts of the country, and it was widely felt that the best way to deal with intruders was to keep them at bay.

It was the arrival of strolling players in Barnstaple which provided the first example of theatre being subsidised from the public purse. When the Earl of Worcester's Players drifted in, they were promptly paid the sum of a few shillings from the local exchequer to move on, without giving any kind of performance, to the next town.

More generous was the reception accorded to the King's Players in 1605. This was the company started by Richard Burbage, of which William Shakespeare had been a member. It was Burbage who produced and promoted most of Shakespeare's plays at the Globe.

What the company performed in Barnstaple or who was in the cast is not recorded in the borough archives. Official records concentrated exclusively on the financial aspects of the occasion. But the event started a legend that Shakespeare himself had strutted the boards at a kind of guildhall situated on Barnstaple Quay, which at that time extended to what is now known as the Strand.

So far as Shakespeare's presence is concerned, it is extremely doubtful whether this is more than folk lore. By 1605 he would have been relatively well-off and even looking forward to retiring back to his native Stratford. It seems unlikely that he would have subjected himself to the obvious discomforts of a South-West tour. That there was a kind of playhouse on the Strand has been supported by researches carried out by Sydney Harper. In his history of Barnstaple, he quotes a record dated 1593 which details the spending of sixpence on the repairs of 'the guildhall roof, caused by Players of the Interlude'.

2

Honeypot Lane to Queen's Hall : 1760s to 1950s

In the 1760s Barnstaple decided to equip itself with a proper theatre. The site chosen was in Honeypot Lane towards the rear of what was later to become the site of the Regal cinema. Nothing remains of the building now except that the passageway leading from High Street to the Strand is known officially as Theatre Lane.

It was at this theatre that one of the greatest English actors of all time was to gain early experience. In 1813 Edmund Kean joined a repertory company operating in Barnstaple under the actor-managership of Henry Lee. Like Garrick before him and Irving, Olivier, and Gielgud, who came later, he specialised in the famous classical roles. He moved on to London and immediately became a celebrity. his Othello and his Richard the Third were soon established quite literally as the talk of the town.

Off stage Kean was somewhat unconventional. It is said that after performing Othello he would stalk out of the theatre without even bothering to remove his make-up and make his way to the nearest tavern. One can imagine the impact on the pub's regulars.

Strangely Kean's sojourn in Barnstaple remains without any form of official commemoration in the town. But that is not so strange when it is remembered that, by and large, there has been similar neglect of the most famous of all Barnstaple's sons, John Gay.

Gay was born in Barnstaple in 1685, his birthplace being premises at the High Street end of Joy Street. He was educated at Barnstaple Grammar School, then situated at St Anne's Chapel in the shadow of

Barnstaple Parish Church.

In 1728 'The Beggar's Opera' established Gay as the Andrew Lloyd-Webber of his day. It was from the start a record-breaking hit. The piece infuriated the then Prime Minister, Sir Robert Walpole, who took its satire on sleaze (bribery and corruption in government circles) to be a reflection on his own administration. He did his best to see that Gay's subsequent work was banned.

Barnstaple would seem to have taken a hint from this censorship. 'The Beggar's Opera' was not staged in Gay's home town until the 1930s, the period of neglect covering over 200 years. Even then, it was an amateur production by the Musical Comedy Society. Gay's most famous work was not presented professionally in the locality until 1953. Far more attention has been paid, for example, to William Frederick Rock.

True, Gay was commemorated by a small repertory theatre established in Newport during the 1930s (more of this will be told later) and his name was given to a road on a local council estate. Some years ago I was involved in a television production on Gay. We visited John Gay Road to find out how many of the residents knew the origin of the name. About two of the people we questioned did so. Others said, 'he was probably an alderman, or something'. At one house we were asked, 'are you from the council and is it about the rent?'

When the Queen's Hall was opened in 1952 I suggested that the name of Gay should be involved in the title. The building was accorded a John Gay Room. In the major reconstruction of the 1990s even this distinction was dropped. The John Gay Room was converted into an upstairs bar.

When the old theatre on Barnstaple Strand, which had seating capacity for 350, ceased to exist in 1833, a more elegant replacement was erected in Boutport Street on a site previously occupied by a row of cottages called 'the Seven Drunkards' because they were in an obvious state of near-collapse. The new building was called the Grecian Hall on account of its architectural design. Later it was renamed The Theatre Royal. Its firsts lessee, named Davis, paid £20 a year for the privilege.

For a while its seasons of entertainment were profitable. But eventually local enthusiasm for live entertainment appeared to fall. By the

1880s the building had become disused. It was even enrolled as a Salvation Army barracks. The advent of moving pictures reactivated its popularity and it was also used for amateur stage productions. It was demolished to make way for a Gaumont cinema in 1931. All that remains to commemorate it now are theatre bills of its plays.

Meanwhile the town had acquired the Albert Hall, built over the old corn market on a corner of Boutport Street adjoining Butchers' Row. This amenity, erected in 1855, was first known as the Music Hall and was intended primarily for concerts, recitals, and other cultural events. The title was none-too-well chosen. Many people would have expected it to star the likes of Marie Lloyd. Music hall was 'the people's entertainment' of the day, and in London it had gained a reputation for sauciness. When Queen Victoria's husband died, reputedly through typhoid caused by the drainage at Buckingham Palace, the Barnstaple building was promptly re-named the Albert Hall.

The theatre Royal and the Albert Hall both played parts in my theatrical grooming. It was at the former that I had my first experience of live theatre. At the age of seven, I was taken by my father to witness a performance by Barnstaple Operatic Society of 'The Yeoman of the Guard'. I promptly fell in love with Elsie Maynard, portrayed by Alice Holmes. I knew the actress slightly in real life for she served in her mother's toy-shop, to which I was a fairly frequent visitor to augment my collection of lead soldiers. There were others in the cast, but I had no eyes for them.

It was at the Albert Hall in 1939 that I reviewed my first play, a performance by a group based on Marwood Rectory and called the Merrywood Players. The play was 'The Middle Watch', a naval comedy by Ian Hay and Stephen King-Hall. The players included an old school friend, John Ray, and Peggy Pearce, with whom I had learned my twice-times table at a prep school run by a headmistress called Miss Mew. Others in the cast, I recall, were Reg Milnes, at that time a popular M C for social events, and John Dixey and Peyto Slatter, whose fathers had both been mayors of Barnstaple. I found it difficult to do more than praise every aspect of the production.

Like the Theatre Royal, the Albert Hall came to be used regularly as a cinema, although it was sometimes hired for amateur stage shows. It ended its activities somewhat spectacularly in 1941. In the second world war it was conscripted as a food store. Some of the food apparently created internal combustion and a fire gutted the building. Its remains served for a period as a British Restaurant, continuing to provide this service until sometime after the end of the war. Then in the early 1950s the Queen's Hall rose like a phoenix on the site.

3

The John Gay Players

No-one realised in the 1930s that Barnstaple was on the verge of a theatrical renaissance. As Neville Chamberlain might have put it, we were emerging from 'Bleak House' into 'Great Expectations'.

During this decade two well-known residents of Barnstaple, J H L Brewer and Bruce Oliver, both actively involved in theatre, had acquired a building in Newport Road, formerly part of a cabinet works, which they intended to develop as a rehearsal room and a kind of arts centre. They named the building after John Gay, conscious of the neglect to which this famous Barumite had been subjected.

The premises had seating accommodation for about 200 and its value to the cultural life of North Devon was established once the second world war had broken out.

Some of the wealthier inhabitants of the Home Counties, fearing immediate air bombardment, sent their families to 'safe areas' of which Barnstaple was considered to be one. These immigrants brought with them Metropolitan tastes and these involved attending the theatre. But in North Devon there was no theatre to attend.

Nature abhors a vacuum, as was proved by subsequent developments. The London theatres were temporarily closed and a number of the smaller companies found themselves without homes.

One such company was the Little Theatre Players, under the leadership of Dorothy Casey and George Wood. Wood had acted with the Royal Shakespeare Company and Dorothy Casey, his wife, had made a reputation in Ireland at the famous Gate Theatre.

They brought with them some accomplished actors: Antony

Massie, who had spent five years in Gielgud's company and was later appointed a lecturer at the Royal Academy of Dramatic Art, Joan Hart, who was to become a member of BBC Repertory Company, Hedley Mattingley, later to feature in the American television series 'Daktari' and other players of similar experience.

Their first production, in the January of 1940, was Ivor Novello's comedy 'Fresh Fields', very much London matinee-audience material. I was commissioned to review it on the first night.

On the following morning I duly submitted my copy and was promptly called into the office of the editor, a leading Methodist. He was unhappy about one aspect of my comment and this was a mention that one of the characters was given the name of Lady Lilian Bedworthy. He questioned whether reference to this fact was suitable in a family journal which had many Nonconformist readers.

As a youngster just emerging from my teens I contested the objection, and after a lengthy argument a compromise was reached. He inserted a note to say that some of the material was not above reproach.

Repertory at the John Gay Theatre had a shaky start, audiences sometimes numbering little more than a dozen, but steadily the public response grew. Between 1940 and 1952 Barnstaple became the smallest town in England supporting its own weekly rep.

Leadership of the company inevitably changed, eventually settling on a triumvirate consisting of Robert Courtney, whose mother ran a business in Barnstaple, Elwyn Evans, from Wales, and Elaine Newell from Ireland. The fare offered consisted mainly of well-established West End successes, such as J B Priestley's 'Dangerous Corner' and 'Duet for Two Hands'. There were talented players in the ensemble, notably Anne Godfrey, Edward Furby, John Waterhouse, Ian Sainsbury, Patricia Leventon, John Packham and Sally Hume.

Miss Godfrey was known locally as 'the type of girl most mothers would like their sons to wed'. Temporary trouble came to her when she was required to appear as a prostitute in a somewhat controversial play. She promptly found herself ignored in public even by people who had previously been fans. One or two tried to convert her from such sinful ways. There was frequent confusion in the minds of the more naive theatregoers between the actors and the characters they portrayed.

It may refresh present memories if I recall others who acted at the John Gay Theatre: Weyman Mackay, Mary Campbell, Richard Harford, Charles Cornock, Ann Gordon, Hettie Senior, Anthony Sheppard, Audrey Munton, and Jennifer Ford. Kenneth Griffiths, at the time a budding film star and now a somewhat controversial documentary writer for television, did a season with the group, reviving his success in 'The Shop at Sly Corner'. Sainsbury later moved into journalism to become the critic of the 'Sheffield Telegraph'. Some of the Courtney-Evans-Newell group are still in the area, these including June Bolam, Audrey Munton, who still undertakes summer seasons with Woolacombe Repertory and Antony Massie, who has retired to the town.

The Wood-Casey group included two old retainers, Mary Campbell and St John Medley. Their contributions sometimes involved unscheduled incidents which had little to do with the script. Medley was reputed to have reached an age when he experienced difficulty in remembering lines. Matters were not improved by the fact that he was somewhat deaf and could rarely hear a prompt. His apparent solution was to decorate the set with cards, each containing words accredited to him. His perambulations on stage from one card to another were carefully followed by patrons who seemed to regret it when such improvisations failed to occur. On one occasion, or so I am told, a stage hand, noting bits of paper littering the props, conscientiously removed the lot. Probably mass confusion was the result.

The John Gay stage had under it a small door, said to have been used when the premises existed as 'a Chinese laundry'. On one occasion, Mary Campbell was required to move through it, but got stuck in the process. It required the services of half the company to pull her out.

Close by the theatre was Coney Gut, a stream which occasionally flooded. On one occasion Hedley Mattingley found his costumes floating beneath the stage, causing panic among the cast.

After his retirement from RADA Antony Massie assisted student theatre at the North Devon College. He also took over the artistic direction of the John Gay Players, staging a production of 'Twelfth Night' which was a commercial as well as a cultural success. His own keen sense of sophisticated humour enabled him to exploit the comedy in the plot. He also created the role of Parson Jack Russell, the famous (or notorious) hunting parson of Swimbridge who became a friend of King Edward the Seventh. Now well into the second half of his eighties he owns to an ambition to have 'one last go' at Shylock. He is encouraged by the fact that on his 90th birthday Sir John Gielgud celebrated the occasion by giving a radio performance of 'King Lear' for the BBC.

REVIEW 1953
(North Devon Journal)

'Twelfth Night'
John Gay Players

The John Gay Players welcome the new Elizabethan era with a comedy by that eminent Old Elizabethan, Mr William Shakespeare, who has virtually monopolised the London theatre during this Coronation year.

From 'Don Juan' to 'Twelfth Night', the new order changes, giving place to old. And if Antony Massie's production lacks the veneer of elegance that characterised the festival week play at Bideford, that is scarcely to be wondered at.

'Don Juan', it is said, cost but a fraction of what is usually spent on a new play in London. 'Twelfth Night' must, of necessity, have cost but a fraction of what was spent on 'Don Juan'.

Nevertheless, it is a competent, concise production, with one or two imaginative touches. There is plenty of frisky horseplay from the comedians and good deal of laughter from both sides of the proscenium arch.

Schoolchildren, who are coming in large numbers, will like the vigorous buffoonery of Peter Sims as Sir Toby; adults will rise more readily to the stylised mobility of Feste, as played by Norman Rose.

Jennifer Ford's Maria is vocal in her acknowledgement of humour. If laughter be the food of comedy, Miss Ford gives us excess of it, but laughter is infectious and it is a pity that the infection spreads to the Duke's court. John Packham's Auguecheek, stockier than tradition would make him, gives us more of the painstaking clown than the mindless fop.

And so to Malvolio, the cross-gartered gull, played with grave dignity by Bruce Stewart, but not with the pomposity necessary to make us rejoice in his humbling. The prank in the garden, therefore, becomes too cruel a business; there is more healthy entertainment in the round-singing of the drunken orgies and in the elaborately promoted duel. The court scenes provide an elegant Orsino from David Palastanga and a poised Olivia from Morag Macnab.

Dominica Clarke's Viola, a performance still to be perfected, is a plucky effort from the youngest member of the cast.

4

The Festival of Britain
& The New Queen's Hall

Once a habit takes root, it spreads and play-going proved no exception. In 1951 Barnstaple decided to celebrate the Festival of Britain and it was agreed that drama should play a major part.

The play chosen was T S Eliot's 'Murder in the Cathedral', depicting the closing stages in the life of Thomas Becket, Archbishop of Canterbury during the reign of King Henry the Second. It terminated with his murder on the altar steps of his own cathedral.

The production was handled by Edward Blacksell, headmaster of Barnstaple Boys' Secondary School and the leading light in Barnstaple Arts Club. Arthur Chandler, the Vicar of Ilfracombe, took on the role of Becket and the performance was given in Barnstaple Parish Church. It drew audiences numbering 1,200 and was later performed to standing room only at the Barn Theatre of Dartington Hall.

But Barnstaple Town Council had acquired an enthusiasm for theatre. They decided to build a playhouse with seating capacity of around 700 on the old Albert Hall site.

The Queen's Hall was duly completed in 1952 and was launched with a performance of '1066 And All That'. It was directed by the theatre's first manager, Edwin Pierce. The reception was somewhat mixed.

Some people stayed away because they objected to the spending of rates on building a theatre when there was still an acute shortage of houses. Many thought that the council's priorities needed to be revised.

Moreover, a legal battle was fought by the promoter of film shows at the old Albert Hall. He claimed that his contract gave him the right to veto live entertainment in the building for a period of five years. In fact, he contended that it was not a new building at all, but the Albert Hall reconditioned. The view of the facade from the street seemed to support that point of view.

He went to the High Court to prove his point and, to the dismay of the council, he won the day. The council took the issue to the Court of Appeal, where again they came out losers. On the third time round, they went to the House of Lords where they gained a victory which was decisive. But many townspeople felt that the cinema proprietor had had less than a square deal. Letters to the Press were numerous and reflected a sharp division of opinion. Even the appearance on the Queen's Hall stage of the Barnstaple-born Harry Welchman, who had gained national fame as the Red Shadow in he London production of 'The Desert Song' (he was hailed at the time as the British answer to Valentino) did little to persuade dissidents to change their minds.

It was under the management of Gordon Kennan that the 'big band sound' echoed through the Queen's Hall. The bookings included such regular and established broadcasters at Ted Heath. By the time he retired in 1976 Kennan had spent 44 years in professional show-business and he did much to create popularity for the building. His successor, Geoffrey Smith, had been general manager of a 3,000 seater Rank Theatre in Cardiff and of Cardiff's Odeon Cinema. He brought to the Queen's Hall not only stars of British variety but Continental companies, Cossack and Rumanian dancers, and even Chinese acrobats. Barnstaple was fortunate to get the Chinese booking. It was one of only twenty venues chosen in a British tour which included Birmingham, Edinburgh, Cardiff, and London. This was indeed a sign that, as a base for theatre, Barnstaple had arrived.

VERSE DRAMA DRAWS OVER 1,500

"Murder in the Cathedral"
Barnstaple Arts Club

Edward Blacksell's production of 'Murder in the Cathedral', presented this week as Barnstaple's dramatic contribution to the Festival of Britain, is simple, imaginative, and powerful and can claim to have moments of real brilliance.

Altogether it has played to audiences of over 1,500 people. Twelve hundred saw it performed on a deep three-tier stage erected over the front pews of Barnstaple Parish Church and the remainder were at the beautiful little Barn Theatre at Dartington Hall, where it drew a capacity house with over 50 standing in the aisles.

Imaginative production is, perhaps, its principal attribute. The interpretation reveals a close understanding of the work, and it is particularly noticeable that in moulding each of the characters into vital and distinct personalities, the producer has to some extent supplemented the impression contained in the text.

It could be argued that this typing has cost the play some of its strength. The priests, for instance, have far too much individuality, but against this must be set the fact that concessions to narrative have undoubtedly helped to interpret the play to the widest of its audiences.

On balance, therefore, innovations can be thoroughly justified, although it is less easy to excuse the unnecessary and distracting gestures of the chorus in the earlier part of the play, and the conference of the knights gains nothing from the histrionics with which it is conducted.

The producer's greatest triumph is in his chorus. It is simply but effectively costumed; it speaks with one voice; it seldom fails to maintain the rhythm of the lines and the grouping, particularly at Dartington, provided a plain and unpretentious atmosphere that blends perfectly with the spirit of the production.

Again simplicity is the keynote of Arthur Chandler's Becket. The humility and strength of the character he produces with deep and sincere feeling, but he applies himself even more skilfully to the subtle task of illustrating, almost surreptitiously, the weakness from within that has to be overcome. Most human of all, he introduces old flashes of arrogance, the legacy of the Cheapside brat, which add immeasurably to the warmth of the character study.

The four tempters have been carefully contrasted: first John Packman, weaving a serpent-like pattern across the stage to propagate the lure of the flesh, then Stanley Thomas, as the quiet, smooth-tongued advocate of the opportunities of court intrigue, then Douglas Blackwell, as the down-to-earth 12th century equivalent of the hard-headed businessman, and finally Thomas Owen, who provides a forceful and dramatic picture of the insidiousness of temptation from within the soul.

5

The Taw & Torridge Festival

Further stimulus for the arts generally, and theatre in particular, in North Devon followed hard on the heels of the opening of the Queen's Hall. Late in 1952 there was talk of the area being made the venue for a national arts festival. Prime movers in the idea were Edward Blacksell, chairman of Barnstaple Arts Club, and Ronald Duncan, a poet and journalist who lived at Welcombe.

Duncan had been more than a minor figure in the revival of poetic drama which followed the end of the second world war. His 'This Way to the Tomb' had achieved a run in London, although being received slightly less enthusiastically than Christopher Fry's 'The Lady's Not For Burning', which had a cast headed by Gielgud and Pamela Brown.

The idea of a North Devon festival caught on with leading personalities in the arts world. among them were Benjamin Britten, widely recognised as the leading British composer of his day, and the distinguished tenor, Peter Pears. There was even a royal involvement in the person of the Earl of Harewood, a grandson of King George the Fifth.

The festival was launched during the summer of 1953. A spectacular programme included a performance by the English Opera company of Gay's 'The Beggar's Opera', set to the music of Britten, which emphasised the Hogarthian element in the plot, and a performance at Bideford (in a cinema converted for the occasion) of Duncan's 'Don Juan'.

Britten and Pears performed at the inaugural concert, which had Lord Harewood as compère. The conductor of 'The Beggar's Opera' was Norman Del Mar. Pears was cast, somewhat improbably, as the

15

highwayman Macheath.

At Bideford 'Don Juan' was directed by E Martin Browne . It was not a work which pleased everyone. A bone of contention was Juan's vow to seduce a bride and a novice before sundown. Bideford at that time was still a Nonconformist town, and such behaviour, even among characters in plays, was not much approved.

The festival programme generally was probably too contemporary for conservative tastes. But many supported it for no better reason than that, because of its social connotations, they could not afford to be left out.

The festival attendances topped 10,000 and it incurred an overall deficit of about £2,000. The result was considered sufficiently satisfactory to continue the project as an annual event.

The success that it achieved owed much to the charm of Lady Harewood, a concert pianist in her own right. Later she was to have a more direct association with North Devon as the wife of Jeremy Thorpe. She became, and still remains, an active inspiration to the local arts scene.

The festival enjoyed widespread national publicity from a development in 1955. To the astonishment of many, the Queen's Hall at Barnstaple was selected for the British premiere of Bertolt Brecht's 'Mother Courage'. Brecht had been for some years a talking point in Europe, not least for his determined defiance of Hitler. In Britain practical experience of his work was substantially unknown.

The play was performed by Joan Littlewood's London company with Miss Littlewood in the title role. The cast included Harry H Corbett, who later gained fame as television's Steptoe Junior. I wanted a picture of him for publication so I contacted a London photographic agent. A photo of Sooty came back by return!

Much of the drama with 'Mother Courage' developed off-stage. Brecht's widow sent emissaries from Germany to get the venture stopped. There was much altercation, but to halt Miss Littlewood when she was set on a purpose was the equivalent of trying to stop a volcano when it was in full eruption. The German dogs barked, but the little caravan moved on.

I saw the first night, along with Harold Hobson and Ken Tynan, two of the most distinguished critics in the country. I was writing notices for 'The Stage' and sundry Devon publications. Tynan was a

Brecht enthusiast and obviously felt that the production did less than full justice to the play. Hobson seemed politely surprised that a remote town in Devon had been chosen for the début.

The festival continued as an annual event for the rest of the decade. It brought to North Devon many celebrities and others who, in due time, were to gain that distinction. Among them was a young man just down from Cambridge called Peter Hall who directed 'The Merchant of Venice' at Barnstaple. He is now one of the august company of theatrical knights.

Sir Laurence Olivier, incidentally, also visited the area, but not for a festival event. He chose to write his autobiography at a hotel in Chittlehamholt. His favourite recreation during his stay was to serve behind the hotel bar. He would sometimes tell customers, 'I'm Laurence Olivier'. Usually they would reply, 'Really? And I'm the Aga Khan'. Village locals were more down to earth. One commented, 'So you're one of these actor fellows. I suppose you take on jobs like this when you're out of work'.

I had the experience of spending a morning in Olivier's company. What impressed me particularly was his genuine interest in the local theatrical scene.

An indirect by-product of the festival was the revitalisation of the Royal Court theatre in London. Blacksell and Duncan were two of the directors of this project. The purpose was to establish in the capital a theatre which would specialise in the work of less than well-established dramatists. Its first big success was with John Osborne's 'Look Back in Anger' which is said to have created the cult of the 'angry young man'. By a coincidence, Osborne had links with North Devon. He was educated at a fee-paying school in Barnstaple, which he left in somewhat sensational circumstances after a stand-up row with the headmaster. He had acted with a repertory company in Ilfracombe.

REVIEW 1957
(North Devon Journal)

SACRED AND INSANE

Play to Challenge the Church

'How can we save Father?' – The English Theatre Company

A sense of continuity is preserved with the Devon Festival drama this year.

Mr Ronald Duncan's 'A Man Named Judas' it may be remembered ended in the disillusioned disciple's taking his life with the aid of a rope. Mr Oliver Wilkinson's 'How Can We Save Father?' opens with a demented cleric contemplating the same method of self-destruction. Only at a national conference of women Conservatives could one expect to find such a constant partiality for the noose. And in other respects the pattern is maintained.

These two festival dramatists have characteristics in common: they share a facility for cloaking serious argument in light banter. Mr Wilkinson would seem, on first inspection, to be the more flippant; it is one thing to make hay with theology as Mr Duncan is sometimes accused of doing; it is quite another to parody Mr T S Eliot (spi-ving and partly spiving, indeed!) as Mr Wilkinson does in his new play.

Battle-cry

But beneath this veneer, his comedy of the curing of a mad parson has an underlying theme; concern for the state of organised religion. And here he sounds a bracing battle-cry for the Church to stir out of its atrophy; to let in the problems of the world; and to forget dogma, so that Christianity may be an active force in life. The sweat-rag - not the collar - must encircle ecclesiastical throats.

Mr Wilkinson's style is contemporary; his characters are symbolic figures, rather than rounded personalities in their own right. That they come to life at all is a triumph for the English Stage Company's young and vigorous players; but Mr John Moffatt's psychiatrist is a power-house generating energy into Mr Peter Wood's production, and Mr John Phillips as the vicar, can maintain an authority even when he is masquerading as a book-end or identifying himself with a cockatoo.

Mr W B Yeats's 'Purgatory' is a mighty atom of a piece which, in the space of fifteen minutes captures something of the titanic tragedy of 'Lear'. Mr Phillips (inaudible at first) plays the father, and Mr Graham Pyle the son. That the echo of Shakespeare should ring so clearly through Mr John Dexter's production is at least partly attributable to Mr Jocelyn Hubert's gaunt and forbidding set.

6

The Beaford Centre

A nother major expansion of artistic and theatrical activity in
North Devon came in 1966, with the establishment of the
Beaford Centre as an offshoot of Dartington Hall.

Dorothy and Leonard Elmhurst – she an American heiress and he
a Yorkshireman who combined practicality with pioneering vision –
had been concerned by a drift of population from the rural areas. In
1925 they bought Dartington Hall as a base for an operation which
would create new industry, linking the process with a corresponding
development in the arts.

To the surprise of many, it proved successful, and by the 1960s
expansion was under consideration. A suitable area seemed to be the
northern territories of the county. Traditionally it had the reputation
of being 'a cultural desert', but the Taw and Torridge Festival, and all
that went with it, might have promoted a revision of this point of
view.

At all events, a move to North Devon was heralded by the establishment in Torrington of Dartington Glass. The next move was to
initiate a service which would encourage an accompanying enthusiasm for the arts.

A somewhat unexpected ally in the development was Jack Oliver,
a colonel in the Territorial Army and a leading administrator in
Devon Rugby Union, excellent qualifications in themselves but not
necessarily those most likely to be associated with the arts. He found
Dartington Trust a headquarters at Greenwarren House in the small
village of Beaford, and thus the Beaford Centre was set up.

The first director was John Lane who had studied at the Slade. He
envisaged a plan which would bring the arts directly to North Devon

doorsteps by organising a regular programme of events in various parts of the area including small villages in which theatre had never once been staged.

The venture was launched ambitiously with a Beaford Festival in which local music and theatre groups took part. An opening season of plays included Pinter's 'The Dumb Waiter', Samuel Beckett's 'Endgame', Anouilh's 'The Rehearsal', Shaw's 'Village Wooing' and Albee's 'The Zoo Story'. The major event brought John Arden to Beaford to act in a play of which he was joint author, 'The Royal Pardon'. Its attack on establishment values was said to epitomise the revolt against convention for which the 1960s are now famed.

By the end of 1966, Beaford had promoted eight plays, fifteen music recitals, six folk concerts, seven art exhibitions, seven film shows and an evening of jazz. By 1970 annual audiences had grown to 25,000. In 1971 the BBC devoted an 'Omnibus' programme to the venture and it was favoured in due course by visits from two ministers of the arts, first Jennie Lee and then Lord Eccles. They both made encouraging noises urging local authorities to increase arts grants.

Public opinion about the whole venture was sceptical. The hard fact remains that John Lane's project is now approaching its thirtieth year. The spring programme for 1995 contains nearly fifty events.

Lane is now no longer in charge of the operation. He remained director at Beaford until 1974 when he was elevated to the board of Dartington Trustees. He is still a resident in Beaford village.

Subsequent Beaford directors have included Harland Walshaw, originally Lane's second in command, Diana Johnson, the first woman to hold the post, Rick Bond, now artistic director at the Queen's Theatre in Barnstaple, and Bob butler, the present Beaford incumbent. They have kept the Beaford wheels turning at a lively pace.

Beaford has also had a succession of popular programme managers. Two I remember particularly are Lise Granados and Shirley Thomas. Lise and I frequently shared a table for events at John Oliver's Lobster Pot on Instow seafront. Sometimes we were joined by George Melly, then film critic of 'The Observer' and at least partly responsible for the revival in Britain of jazz.

Shirley Thomas was the daughter of one of North Devon's leading cattle breeders, famous throughout the country and in South America for his bulls. She combined her artistic activities with practical work on his Umberleigh farm.

Not the least of Beaford's achievements has been to stimulate activity in other local organisations promoting various branches of the arts, including theatre. It has also brought many touring professional theatre groups into the area and this has done much to raise theatrical tastes.

7

The Orchard Theatre

Two branches of Beaford activities have made enormous contributions to the enrichment of theatre in North Devon. In 1969 a group of students just down from E15 drama school decided that they wished to spend a period continuing to work together as a group.

Among them was Andrew Noble, the son of a hotelier in the Ilfracombe area and well acquainted with the history of Barnstaple's involvement with professional rep.

He discussed with me as an idea whether repertory could be revived in the town. My advice was that weekly rep was a non-starter, particularly since funding agencies were no longer interested in theatrical ventures which involved rehearsing one play, presenting another, and learning a third, all in the space of the same week.

But we agreed that there might be a future for a company which would tour productions - probably half-a-dozen per year - to the principal towns of Devon and Cornwall. We also surmised that John Lane would not be adverse to adding a repertory group to his rapidly expanding artistic empire. Noble took the hint and made an approach, and thus the Orchard Theatre was created.

Cynics gave it a life expectation of about six months. In 1994 it celebrated its silver jubilee and it has become one of the longest-established and most successful touring theatres in the south of England.

Its first production at the Queen's Hall was Harold Brighthouse's 'Hobson's Choice', a classic among north country comedies. Actors in the venture, as well as Noble, were Evadne Stevens, Peter Dansiger, John Hartley, David Atkinson, and Sarah Stephenson, to be joined fairly promptly by Fleur Chandler.

Hartley went on to join the Royal Shakespeare Company, return-ing to Barnstaple with it in 1980, when 'King Henry the Fourth' was performed. Noble later became a lecturer in drama at a Florida uni-versity and then director of the New Zealand equivalent of RADA in Wellington. Miss Stephenson achieved national publicity when she played Desdemona in a production of 'Othello' by Sir Bernard Miles. It centred on the fact that her death scene was performed in the nude.

The Orchard enjoyed its share of controversy on the Home Front. One argument arose from a performance of Joe Orton's 'Loot'. I enjoyed the play's black humour and commended it in my notice. I was promptly attacked by a member of the Moral Rearmament Campaign. His objection, so far as I could gather, was that I recom-mended the play, with its challenge to establishment values, for the attention of schools.

The Orchard, in early days, featured a few plays involving charac-ters noted in local history, some written by members of the team. John Hartley wrote 'Richard Neville of Bideford'. Trevor Heddon contributed 'Cruel Coppinger', the story of one of the most ruthless and brutal smugglers operating along the Hartland coast.

As confidence grew, Orchard activities extended to Shaw's 'Pygmalion' (some playgoers thought it was a new and straight ver-sion of 'My Fair Lady' and regretted that the songs had been cut) and Ian Fell's adaptation of 'Lorna Doone'.

The Orchard even took on the role of investigative journalists to test public opinion on the building of a link road from Barnstaple to the M5. John Wilkey combined their findings in a drama called 'The Road to the West'.

New faces had arrived on the Orchard scene. Among them was Richard Griffiths, who has since become a television star through his role as a detective inspector in 'Pie in the Sky'. I remember particu-larly his Good Fairy Liquid in an Orchard Christmas show. He was always a man of considerable girth. When he appeared in Brecht's 'Galileo' in London, gossip columnists put his weight at 18 stone.

James Walker created a reputation with local audiences for his one-man interpretation of Dickie Slader, the pedlar-poet of Molland Cross. I saw the performance on the edge of Exmoor where some members of the audience knew Slader personally. They reckoned that

Walker had got his mannerisms just right.

The Orchard have been fortunate in their recent directors, Paul Chamberlain, Nigel Bryant, and Bill Buffery, who formerly produced for the Royal Shakespeare Company. Chamberlain introduced the work of such Westcountry authors as Allen Saddler, a South Devon critic, C P Taylor and Nick Darke. This tradition has been sustained by Bill Buffery. His early 1995 production was 'Plantation' by the Exeter writer John Pilkington. The principal character was played by Gill Nathanson, who once taught drama at Pilton School.

Another Orchard tradition which has been sustained has been the inclusion in each annual programme of at least one Shakespeare play. Probably the most popular was 'Twelfth Night', with John Surman as Malvolio. It held second place in the Orchard table of box-office successes, being surpassed only by Thomas Hardy's 'Far From the Madding Crowd', an adaptation of the novel which was the work of Sally Hedges, Nigel Bryant's wife.

Orchard actors who have established firm local followings include Matthew Solon, who has written television scripts for Penelope Keith; Donal McBride; Heather Brechin; and Michelle Magorian, who developed a one-woman show in mime.

Bill Buffery's first work in theatre, after coming down from Oxford, was as a nymph in 'The Tempest', when his fellow sprites included Juliet Stephenson and Ruby Wax. When he produced the play for the Orchard in 1992, he played a particularly vicious Caliban to John Surman's Prospero. Andrea Gascoigne doubled Miranda with Ariel, a fairly daring innovation. She flitted from one role to the other, indicating her change of identity merely through the removal of her skirt.

REVIEW 1969

(North Devon Journal)

Joe Orton slaughters sacred cows

'Loot' – The Orchard Theatre Company

The late and much lamented Joe Orton was a dramatist who had a reputation for making his comedies blacker than black.

In one respect, the Orchard performance of 'Loot' at the Lobster Pot on
Monday contained an element of anti-climax.

I attended expecting that my sense of decency would be raped with
every second line in the dialogue, I departed feeling that I had witnessed
one of the most wholesomely funny British farces since 'Charley's Aunt'.

Admittedly, the humour in 'Loot' is bizarre; it ranges around such subjects as corpses, coffins, and funerals; and strange as it may seem in a
Christian country, there are still many Englishmen who shy away from
jokes involving the trappings of death.

'Loot' violates no less enthusiastically other long-established taboos;
those which surround Holy Church, the Crown and the peculiar but cher-
ished fallacy that the Police can do no wrong.

None of this seems to be in the slightest degree offensive. I would rate
'Loot' less of an affront to public taste than, for example, 'Arsenic and Old
Lace,' which most right-minded people would regard as a singularly harm-
less play.

Authority in contempt

And Mr Orton is more than a mere slaughterer of sacred cows. His contempt for the divine right of Authority has the ring of sincerity, but he can
express it with a brilliant turn of phrase.

If I had to define his particular genius, I would say that it lies in his
ability to clothe ludicrous and outrageous situations in language which is
formal, elegant and refined.

Thus does the devout Roman Catholic nurse, a young woman staunch
in her Faith who makes a habit of murdering her patients for personal
gain, describe the evangelical bank robber son of the household.

'His dressing-table is decorated, not only with firearms but with family-
planning equipment. A Papal dispensation is needed before I can dust his
room.'

There is another inspired moment when Andy Noble, as the son, standing by the body of his mother as it awaits burial and ruminating rhythmi-
cally on the wonders of the Spanish bordellos, beats out a castanet
accompaniment with her false teeth.

Charles Lewson's production sustains the pace admirably with excellent portrayals by John Hartley, as the detective, and Peter Dansiger as
the undertaker. Sarah Stevenson's nurse is by far the best work she has
yet done for the Orchard.

If this piece belonged to any one actor the claim must be made on behalf of Mr Hartley's corrupt and bullying law-enforcement officer. ('It is expedient that the general public should not have the confidence of the Police undermined,' he says, as he repeatedly strikes the miserable youth he is questioning).

Mr Hartley, solid and self-satisfied, and as well-lined with capon as was Shakespeare's Justice, embodies the serious theme behind Orton's flippancy: that in a materialistic society the motivating force is greed.

§

REVIEW 1971
(North Devon Journal)

Up to the neck in mortality

'Happy Days' – The Orchard Theatre Company

In Harland Walshaw's production at the Lobster Pot on Friday, Samuel Beckett's 'Happy Days' was seen to be a warm, beautiful, and emotionally involving play.

This was an achievement for Mr Walshaw and his cast; the piece could so easily have failed to communicate, leaving its audience bewildered and unmoved.

Its quality was brought to light in a performance of some brilliance by Evadne Stevens, who spent the evening slowly subsiding into a mound of yellow earth.

When the story opened, she was already buried up to her waist. At the close, as old-age gripped her character of Winnie, all that remained visible of her was her head.

By this means does Beckett confront us with one of the fundamental truths of life; that from the moment of birth we begin the process of gradual death.

Another profound truth emerges as Winnie is steadily sucked under; that we are all solitaries, condemned to make our own way in the world.

Desperate chatter

As the earth level rises, Winnie maintains a desperate flow of chatter, delivered in the direction of her husband, Willie.

But Willie spends most of the time concealed in a burrow, emerging only occasionally to offer a monosyllabic reply or to quote irrelevant snippets from the Sunday Press.

The rapport between them is almost non-existent, yet when it functions Winnie's face lights up with an expression of indescribably joy.

It was here - in the conveyance of this sense of joy, this inner radiance which found hope in a situation bordering on despair - that Miss Stevens carried the play through as a meaningful experience.

For Beckett, although he sees human existence in dour terms, is not entirely a pessimist. He is prepared to concede that Man has been given a natural aptitude to find sustenance in faith.

And Miss Stevens's Winnie, welcoming each new day and the isolation which attends it, revealed something of what theologians mean when they speak of the peace of God.

Martin Harris's Willie did all that was required to offset one of the finest individual performances that we have yet seen in an Orchard tour.

§

(North Devon Journal)
REVIEW 1973

A touch of the Monty Pythons

'The wonderful Adventure of Baron Munchausen' – The Orchard Theatre

And now for something completely different, the Orchard's contribution to the seasonal festivities is pantomime devised with the Monty Python touch.

Almost anything can happen in John Wilkie's adaptation of the legend of Baron Munchausen.

Cannon fire, atom bombs explode, whales disgorge principal boys, monsters come to life, massed bands and choirs break in for no obvious reason and the Post Office Tower restaurant is sent spinning across the stage.

The villain, an archduke with a power complex, who wants to dominate Europe by stealing all nine of the Common Market charters, even masquerades briefly as Edward Heath.

Strange and wonderful effects are introduced though film, shadowgraph, and any-to-come glad-of-it. It is fair to say that the show is at odds with all conventional conceptions of theatre. But one senses the freedom achieved in this liberation.

A magnificent red horse is paraded, and it does not seem in the least degree incongruous that the actor playing the back legs should suddenly emerge from his covering to join in an argument. Nor is it disconcerting when, in the middle of a scene, a stage hand emerges with a broom to sweep up the floor.

Bizarre humour

Some of us first encountered this style of humour with 'Hellsapoppin.' Then came the Goons, and, more recently, the Flying Circus. The patterns in 'Munchausen' are scarcely less bizarre.

But it is not all nonsense; Mr Wilkey can write a good romantic song as easily as he develops a rock session and he can deal sincerely with issues like true love.

Nevertheless, the show is made for me by Richard Griffiths's Good Fairy Liquid, a cross between Beryl Reid and Benny Hill. James Walker times his way immaculately through the role of the Baron, and Alan Butler is satisfyingly diabolical as the Archduke. Heather Brechin's principal boy is rural Devonian, and the heroine, whose 'daddy is a baddie,' is made naturally appealing by Frances Crane.

More music would not come amiss. The sources of such as there is range from the classics to commercial television jingles. Andrew Noble directs, with Nick Gardner as 'knee-wobbler extraordinary.' The musicians are David Cawthra, Richard Diwell, and Robert Bright.

§

REVIEW 1983
(North Devon Journal)

Gay turned Savage

'The Threepenny Opera' – Orchard Theatre Company,
North Devon College Arts Centre

Paul Chamberlain's swan-song in North Devon - his production of Brecht's 'The Threepenny Opera' - comes as a fine climax to five years' work.

His grip on the play is firmer than that which he exerted on 'The Beggar's Opera' when he revived that for the John Gay revel five weeks ago.

Brecht based his plot on Gay's using the same characters in a broadly identical story but setting it in near-contemporary Soho.

What the two Orchard performances have demonstrated is the difference of mood in the two lines of approach.

Bitter

Gay's satire was seen to be mischievous rather than vicious.

No doubt at all was left that Brecht's was intended as a bitter indictment of mankind and of the economic system under which, in the Western world, it chooses to live.

The clarity of the message owed much to Cliff Atkinson's interpretation of the Kurt Weill music.

The atmosphere was established during the first few seconds, through Ken Sabberton's savage delivery of the theme song.

The words emerged like a searing burst of machine-gun fire, decimating resistance to an argument which, judging by the polls, Britons generally have no overwhelming desire to hear.

For Mac the Knife, Simon Slater cultivated the manners and accent of a lower middle class London upstart, the back-street boy who, in a corrupt society, has discovered how money can be made.

The portrayal was as brutal as Gay's Macheath is traditionally made romantic. No sympathy was courted, at least at surface level.

There was, of course, cynicism underlying the contention that the Christian duty of all solid citizens is to have such villains, steeped in the technique of rape and murder, hanged by the neck until they are dead.

Brecht tells British reactionaries, in effect, to take stock of their own position in relation to their tacit support for Facist regimes overseas.

John Surman, the best character-actor that the Orchard have acquired since the days of Richard Griffiths and James Walker, made the bent police chief sentimental and loathsome, a self-contained examination of hypocrisy, and sinister bonhomie radiated from the Peachum of Ian Good.

Earthy

Mary Roscoe's Polly sang well, was pleasantly earthy, and revealed a working girl's shrewdness and honesty of purpose.

Roz Clifton was a practical and thoroughly amoral Mrs Peachum, Katy Feeney a cool Jenny Diver, and Sonia Ritter a hot-blooded and formidable Lucy.

The Lucy-Polly conflict had similarities, although placed at a lower level of breeding, with that created for Gwendolen and Cecily by Oscar Wilde.

The company double up effectively as spivs, petty gangsters and whores, and Mick Dunk signs an economic but visually satisfying set.

§

REVIEW 1986
(North Devon Journal)

Mozart's Abanazer

'Amadeus' – Orchard Theatre Company

Nigel Bryant's production of 'Amadeus' finds the Orchard in the form which has placed it among the major theatre companies of the South West.

Peter Shaffer's story of Mozart is, indeed, exceptional material. The cinema version has won a chain of international awards. And, as is invariably the case, the play is more satisfying than the film.

The tale is told by Mozart's arch-rival Salieri, who devoted himself to promoting the downfall of the young genius.

Gargantuan

It is a gargantuan role, which keeps the actor on stage for all of two-and-a-half hours, and John Surman, like a wicked uncle in panto, turns it into a veritable tour de force.

Infinitely devious, he delivers a visual sermon on the theme of envy, handled with subtlety and in tongue-in-cheek style.

Legend credits Salieri with the poisoning of Mozart. But the poison is seen to be, not arsenic, but sheer malevolence masquerading as friendship. And ultimately it destroys both men.

Highlights in the portrayal include Salieri's exasperation on discovering that Mozart is a Mason. This, he suspects, will protect his potential victim from the worst excesses of the plotting against him. What Freemasonry

29

did for Mozart, of course, was to inspire 'The Magic Flute'.

Martin Stone, in the title part, is youthful, enthusiastic, arrogant, and much given to lavatorial humour. He exudes the charm which evidently seduces most of his female pupils, and does it all with an air of childlike innocence. He is, in essence, a bawdy Peter Pan.

Bottom-drawer

Rebecca Harbord contributes a lively and practical Constanze, humorous, good hearted, loyal and socially out of the bottom drawer.

The other characters are filled by David Stevens, Brendan Barry, Graham Coleclough, and Jonathan Milton, the last-mentioned as the Emperor Joseph II, whose respect for money earned him the nickname 'Kaiser Keepit'. Appropriately, perhaps, Mr Milton has an honours degree in economics.

Stella Searson plays keyboards and Sally Hedges researched the music. The set, by Rodney Ford, consists of transparent screens in the shape of harps.

§

REVIEW 1991
(North Devon Journal)

Puck goes punk

'A Midsummer Night's Dream' – Orchard

The magic of Oberon, often tinged with malice, may well have caused the premiere of the Orchard's 'A Midsummer Night's Dream' to be staged in weather more suited to 'The Snow Queen'.

The first night was nevertheless notable, and for three distinct reasons.

It initiated the company's 21st year; it marked the North Devon debut of the director, Bill Buffery as an actor; and it caused all three sides of the Plough's auditorium to be brought into use.

Hard on the ear

The extension of the seating had its shortcomings, for audibility occasionally suffered.

Mr Buffery's own delivery rose splendidly to the challenge. His Oberon, if not markedly authoritative, had more sensitivity than is often attributed to the character. Mary Woodvine's Titania was at least a match for him in the verbal in-fighting.

The partnership was extended to cover Theseus and Hippolyta and here Miss Woodvine made a duchess of magnificently Amazonian blood.

The play has frequently suffered through the prettification of its attendant fairies. Mr Buffery had none of this nonsense. Cobweb, Mustardseed, and Co, were not a gang that one would have cared to encounter while strolling through an enchanted wood.

I was less than entirely happy with Tristan Sturrock's punk Puck, plebeian in accent and wearing red boots and braces and a string vest, with a ring decorating his ear and a hairstyle to match.

His attributes included spectacular agility, a quality also evident in he spirited Hermia of Andrea Gascoigne and the well-matched Helena of Katy Stephens. Anthony Askew's Lysander and Daniel Bentley's Demetrius could never hope to be more than supporting roles.

The mechanicals wore factory-floor overalls, with Alistair Findlay as a harassed Quince and John Surman as a Bottom more subtle than boisterous in his efforts to get his own way.

It was a sign of the times that two of the rustics were female. This part of the plot blossomed in Pyramus and Thisby, given an oriental touch.

Meg Surrey's set was impressively regal and her forest contained some of those mysterious fairy rings.

§

REVIEW 1994
(North Devon Journal)

Orchard's Chekov hit
'Uncle Vanya' – Orchard Theatre Company

After a leanish nine months, Orchard Theatre is promising an appropriate climax to its silver jubilee year.

It is now touring 'Uncle Vanya', to be followed promptly by excerpts from Alan Bennett's 'Talking Heads'.

Bill Buffery's handling of the Chekov must rank among his finer achievements in the area. It eschews completely the cloying whimsy which has cluttered many British productions of the author in the past.

Buffery himself contributes a study of the conservationist Astrov, despairing of what Big Business is doing to Nature and haunted by a realisation that the love of his life can never be fulfilled. He portrays the role with a sense of smoothness and style.

Self-indulgent

John Surman's Serebriakov, a self-indulgent academic maintained by relatives in his ivory castle, has touches of the high comedy for which he is well known.

Gill Nathanson's Sonia, inhibited by an unfounded belief that she lacks sex-appeal, has innate sensitivity. Thomasina Unsworth's Yelina, frustrated in an unsatisfactory marriage, arouses sympathy with a sharper touch.

Ian Bailey's Vanya simmers with indignation, eventually erupting like a volcano. Zoe Hicks, David Plimmer, and Veda Warwick give thorough support in a performance which makes a Czarist Russian period piece into a play for today.

1   *'Charley's Aunt' – Brandon Thomas. The Friends Dramatic Society. Simon Blacksell, Richard Quick, Suzanne Snell, Michael Reynolds. The Queen's Hall.*

As FHK points out (see ch.12) amateur theatre kept theatre in general alive in North Devon during its lean years. All our photographs are, therefore, strictly local; either of amateur societies' work, or of the John Gay Company (very rare archive material), or the Orchard, our own locally based professional Company (see ch. 6 & 7).

This choice of photographs does not undervalue professional visitors like the Royal Shakespeare Company or Footsbarn, but shows, rather, how a lively local pro/am interaction may reflect and complement the wider theatrical scene.

2   *'The Merry Wives of Windsor' – Wm. Shakespeare. The Friends Dramatic Society. Betty Worwood, Janet Potter, Jack Westcott. The Queen's Hall.*

3   *'Little Women' – Louisa M. Alcott.*

Joan Hart, Antony Massie, Frances Lovering, Charles Cornock, George Wood & Dorothy Casey (1940).

'Little Women' was at the John Gay Theatre (now a car show-room) in Newport Road (see ch. 3).

The Arts Club was the leading influence in the setting up of the Taw & Torridge Festival (see ch. 4 & 5). These photographs indicate that the up-to-dateness of the Provinces is perhaps too easily be-littled. 'Little Women' is still going strong, albeit in the cinema; and the Royal Court, born in North Devon (see ch. 5) is having a completely refurbished theatre.

4   *Members of the Barnstaple Arts Club at an Arts Club Ball.*

Joan Blacksell, Brian Chugg, 'Newki' & Queenie Newcombe, Edward Blacksell, June (Bolam) Sainsbury.

5   *The Barum Players MUSIC HALL team.*

Back Row: Kenneth James, Reg Ash.
Front Row: Fracie Ash, Graham Sargent, Josephine Worth,
George Addy, Rene Addy. (Producer Kenneth James).

The Barum Players (see ch. 16) did sterling work in the 50s &
60s keeping alive local interest in the theatre. Josephine
Worth also played leads for the Musical Comedy Society (see
ch. 13). The juxtaposition of these photographs is a pleasing
reminder of the variety of theatrical fare that has long been
available to North Devon audiences and of the range of productions that FHK reviewed.

6   *'The Zoo Story' – Edward Albee.*

Peter Davey & Chris Jones produced by Janet Potter for the
Friends Dramatic Society (1965).

7   *'Endgame' – Samuel Beckett.*

Peter Davey & Patrick Cotter as Clov & Hamm (1966).

Much of Beaford's early drama (see ch. 6 & 7) like 'Endgame', before the advent of the Orchard (see ch. 6 & 7), was amateur work. 'Endgame' was produced for the first Beaford Festival. The Orchard goes from strength to strength, and one of their strengths is John Surman who was in Bill Bufferey's 1995 'Doll's House'.

---

8   *'Uncle Vanya' – Tchekhov'*

Zoë Hicks (Marya), John Surman (Serebriakov). Orchard Theatre (1994).

John Marks at Ilfracombe & North Devon College has introduced student and adult performers (and their audiences) to a range of plays, from Feydeau & Coward to the great Greek dramatists of the 5th century BC (see ch. 9, 10 &15). Hermione Gulliford played Clytemnestra in the 'Orestaia'. She & J-AB are now working actresses.

10   *'The Young Idea'* – *Noel Coward.*

Eve Marie Wells & Sean Kempton. Open Theatre (Apprentices) North Devon College (1991).

9   *'A Flea In Her Ear'* – *Feydeau,*

Hermione Gulliford, Julie-Alanah Brighten, Sean Kempton. Open Theatre (Apprentices) North Devon College (1990).

11   *'The Cherry Orchard' – Tchekhov.*

The Open Theatre at North Devon College. Hamish Patrick & Paula Morante.

Two Tchekhov productions, one directed by John Marks at North Devon College, and the other by Daphne Lock at Ilfracombe College (see ch. 9, 10 & 15) indicate that enterprising local amateur work is a valuable complement to our excellent Queen's Theatre programmes (see ch. 21).

12   *'Wild Honey' – Tchekhov.*

The Company, Studio Theatre at Ilfracombe College.

Donald MacCallam has acted with John Marks & Chris Jackson at Ilfracombe College (see ch. 9. 10 & 15) and with the Friends DS (see ch. 4). His most recent appearance was in Tchekhov's 'the Three Sisters' at Ilfracombe . Chester Lovering, both as a performer (see ch. 12&13) and preceding John Marks at North Devon College, has done most interesting work, notably presenting Tennessee Williams's plays at NDC. The 'Streetcar' photograph is of the late Terry Jones' touring production in 1965.

13   'The Duchess of Malfi' – John Webster.

Donald MacCallam & Katie Jones. Studio Theatre, Ilfracombe College (1990)

14   'A Streetcar Named Desire' – Tennessee Williams.

Chester Lovering & Sandra Squires at the North Devon College (1965)

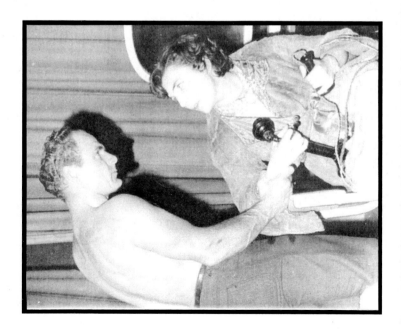

Chris Jackson at Ilfracombe with the Studio Theatre (see Ch. 9, 10 & 15), has followed a challenging road (for 10 years now), not being confined to the Classics, but venturing also into the more controversial modern field. The Operatic Society (see ch. 13) has a long and successful record of productions. Light Opera and Musical Comedy are the 20th Century's special contribution to the Theatre. The 30 year gap between the first 3 Opera photographs and those following (in the centrefold) is evidence of the long-running musical activity of the Society.

16   *'The Beggar's Opera.* – *John Gay.*

The Barnstaple Operatic Society. Lillian Dallyn, Alfred Jeffery, Dorothy Dart & Minnie Joint (1938).

15   *'The Entertainer'* – *John Osborne.*

Larry Fabian. Studio Theatre at Ilfracombe College (1992).

17   *'The Mikado' – Gilbert & Sullivan.*

Minnie Joint, Alice Holmes, Gladys Richards (1929). At the (then) Albert Hall.

18   *'Utopia Unlimited' – Gilbert & Sullivan.*

John Brewer, Minnie Joint, Gladys Richards (1930). At the (then) Albert Hall.

19   'Rosemarie' – Rudolf Friml & Herbert Stothart.

Chester Lovering & Sandra Squires (1962). At the Queen's Hall.

20   'The Gondoliers' – Gilbert & Sullivan.

Mary Chant, Tom Stirzaker, Simon Speed Andrews, Diane Bosence, Michael Davey (1993). At the Queen's Hall.

21   *'The Toreador'*

Unknown, Minnie Joint, George Worth, Bruce Oliver. The Musical Comedy Society (1929).

The Barnstaple Musical Comedy Society (see ch. 13) is presenting this year (1995) 'Anything Goes', the Cole Porter musical, at the now Queen's Theatre. These early photographs show not only the long theatrical life of the Society, but also the contribution of the old Albert Hall to the community (see ch. 2 & 21).

22   *'The Shop Girl'*

Mary Clay, Mrs. (Doctor) Thomas, George May, Minnie Joint (1930). At the (then) Albert Hall.

THE TOREADOR

THE SHOPGIRL 1930

23   The Barnstaple Musical Society's Company in 'Veronique' at the Albert Hall (1936).

From 'Veronique' to 'the Dancing Years' to 'Kiss Me Kate' is a splendid continuity for the Musical Comedy Society (see ch. 13). The hats worn by the Ladies of the Orchestra in 'Veronique' are especially eye-catching. The 'Veronique' photograph is from Mr. Ockie Potier's magnificent album of the production.

24   'Kiss Me Kate' – Cole Porter.

The Company in 1972 at the Queen's Hall.

As well as recording the longevity of musical theatre in North Devon, our photographs are also a history of 'the theatrical photograph' – almost no one uses publicity material like this today.

25   *'The Dancing Years' – Ivor Novello.*

The Company at the Queens Hall (1965).

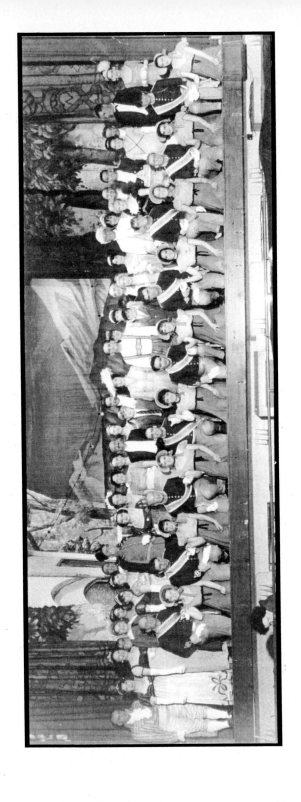

26   *'The Importance of Being Earnest' – Oscar Wilde.*

The Friends Dramatic Society (1962). Betty Worwood, Jack Westcott, June (Bolam) Sainsbury. The Queen's Theatre.

The Friends Dramatic Society (see ch. 14) staged their first production in 1960 – 'Twelfth Night'. The last was 'Lady Windermere's Fan' (Wilde) in 1978, though Ann Westcott directed Ibsen's 'Ghosts'; 'What the Butler Saw' (Orton); 'Hamlet'(Shakespeare); and 'Death of a Nightingale' (Timberlake Wertenbaker) in the late 80s/ early 90s for John Marks at North Devon College (see ch. 9, 10. & 15).

27   *'The Winter's Tale' – Wm. Shakespeare.*

The Friends Dramatic Society. Angela Ford & Chris Jones. The Queen's Theatre.

28   'King's Rhapsody' – Ilfracombe Operatic Society.

Eileen Candy & Charles Price, directed by Ted & Marie Eley at the Alexandra Theatre. Early 1960s.

The Ilfracombe Operatic Society (see ch. 16) had a valuable career, but succumbed to the pressures of rising costs & the difficulties of venue (see ch. 15). Eileen Candy played a delightful Polly for the Friends DS (see ch. 14) in 'Beggar's Opera'. The Ilfracombe Pantomime Society (see ch. 16) has just celebrated its 10th anniversary, which is a splendid achievement, considering the competition both from Plymouth & the excellent Queen's Theatre pantomimes.

---

29   The Principals in Pam Beacham's first Pantomime for the Ilfracombe Pantomime Society, 'Jack and Jill' (1985).

Paula Stairmand (tragically killed in a car accident), Ron Rhodes, Pat Johnson and Malcolm Robinson.

30   The Braunton Productions' Company in 'Fiddler on the Roof'.

Tony Evans as Tevye is on the left.

The St. Giles, Tradishaw, and Torrington Players (see ch. 20) are actually almost a continuum, demonstrating FHK's view that the theatre is able endlessly to renew itself. The GBS piece was performed for the Beaford Opening Festival (see ch. 6).

Braunton Productions (see ch. 16) is a group that has survived (since 1974) by offering lively, slightly unusual productions, and having, like the Barnstaple Musical Society, a 'junior' section. FHK rated Braunton's 'Hello Dolly' very high.

31   'A Village Wooing' – George Bernard Shaw.

The Tradishaw Players. John Bailey & Molly Hillyer (1966).

32   The St. Giles Players' Company in 'The Happiest Days of Your Life' (1958).

Chapter 20 traces the network of theatrical clerics and their associated productions, which are a truly astonishing collection of exotic work, including Bridie's 'Tobias and the Angel' and Ben Travers' 'Rookery Nook'. Out of this network and this rich theatrical mix, the St. Giles, the Torrington, and the Tradishaw Players sprang, though FHK only records the Tradishaws. Woolacombe Repertory has achieved 25 years of Summer Seasons at Hall 70, Woolacombe. Members of the Company have acted with other Groups out-of-Season.

33   'Blithe Spirit' – Noel Coward.

Woolacombe Repertory. Wendy Morrall, Dorothy Pile, Jillian Rowe (1981). Woolacombe Hall 70.

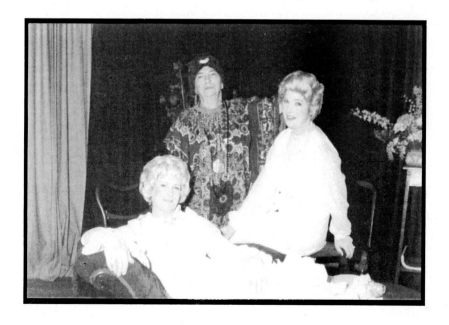

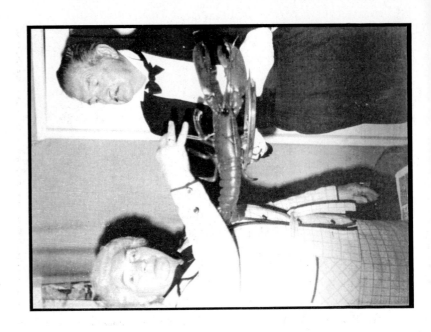

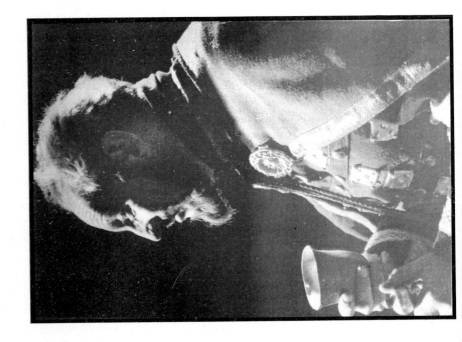

34   *'The Hollow' – Agatha Christie. Woolacombe Repertory Players, 1979. Dorothy & Tom Pile.*

These last two photographs exemplify the interconnections of local players and theatres (professional and amateur), that have helped to keep, and one hopes will continue to keep, theatre active in what is still fundamentally a rural area, unrecognised by Whitehall. The wider the net of pro/am involvement, the higher the production standards (see ch.22) and the likelier an interested and informed audience. Happy examples of this amateur/professional link are Andy Noble & Gill Nathanson (see ch. 7) & Janet Dale (see ch. 8), as are Esmé Preston's successes (see ch.11).

All the Pile family (see ch. 17) were members of Equity. Tom & Dorothy Pile directed 'Die Fledermaus' and 'the Vagabond King' for the Barnstaple Operatic Society (see ch. 12); and 'the Beggar's Opera' for the Friends DS (see ch. 14).

Chester Lovering & Sandra Squires were in 'Vagabond' as were David Rigby and Jack Westcott. John Chilcott (see ch. 16) was MacHeath and Jack Westcott Peachum (in 'Beggar's Opera').

All these productions were at the Queen's Hall (see ch. 2, 4 & 21) which the Operatic, the Musical Comedy, Braunton Productions and the Dance Schools (see ch. 11) still use.

35   *'Macbeth' – Wm. Shakespeare. David Rigby for the Friends Dramatic Society, 1963. The Queen's Hall.*

8

The Plough, Torrington

E ven as recently as 1970, few residents of Torrington, a small market town with a population of around 3,000, envisaged that within half a decade it would be equipped with a well furnished theatre of its own.

The likes of John Lane had other ideas. Their determination to raise the level of cultural activity in the locality caused them to look expectantly in the direction of the Plough.

The Plough, an ancient tavern, occupied a prime site in the town centre. It had been used as a local drill hall but, as enthusiasm for military training had declined, it had fallen into disuse. It had been called 'a white elephant' at a meeting of the town council during the winter of 1972.

The arts fraternity promptly stepped in with the suggestion of a £12,000 conversion scheme which would turn the building into a theatre - cum cinema -cum art gallery.

Torrington Rural Council were initially none too enthusiastic. They obviously viewed the spending as an extravagance. But by the following year they had negotiated a £76,000 tender for the first phase of the work.

Some sections of local opinion were full of misgivings. If large sums of public money were to be spent, they felt, a heated swimming pool would be of more benefit to the youth of the town. They were not much comforted by an estimate that the arts project could be expected to lose £5,000 a year. Torrington Cavaliers, the promoters of spectacular events in the area, even demanded a referendum to test public attitudes to the idea.

Plans for the Plough nevertheless went ahead. Torrington Town

Council put up £75,000 and there was further backing from the Arts council, the Gulbenkian Foundation, the British Film Institute, Torrington Rural Council, and the English tourist Board.

By 1975 the Plough was ready to fulfil its new role and it was announced that Dame Edith Evans, then aged 87, would make a 250-mile journey to be in at the official birth. Everyone knew of Dame Edith, if only because of her delivery of the famous 'handbag' line in 'The Importance of Being Earnest'. If a celebrity of her standing could give the development her personal support, it was felt, it should not be in the nature of generous-minded Torringtonians to hold back.

Not that Dame Edith was too impressed with the Plough layout, which suggested a kind of cockpit stage with seating on three sides. Gazing at a capacity house, she demanded in the most august of tones that her voice could command, 'how can I be expected to speak in three directions at the same time?'

Her programme included reminiscences, readings, and extracts from plays in which she had been featured. It was richly embellished by stories of the famous players whom she had partnered. It heralded an opening festival which was to last from March until May.

A programme in honour of the occasion included a new musical work, 'East of the Sun, West of the Moon', written by the composer-in-residence at the Beaford Centre, Andrew Harvey. Major Road Theatre Company presented John Spurling's 'On a Clear Day You Can See Marlowe' and the Orchard Theatre staged 'The Ballad of the Artificial Mash'. Film revivals included 'King Kong', and 'Modern Times', the latter as a tribute to Sir Charles Chaplin. George Melly, with Johnny Shilton and the Feetwarmers, and the local Soloheim Mungash group represented jazz. There were slots for Holsworthy Theatre Company, Torrington Drama Workshop and Bideford School Drama Group and the Plough was incorporated in the town's traditional May Fair events.

In 1978 it became the venue for the first visit to North Devon by the Royal Shakespeare Company. Sir Ian McKellan headed a cast which performed 'Twelfth Night' and 'The Three Sisters'.

Another distinguished visitor was Alan Ayckbourn, who directed personally a performance of 'Joking Apart' by his own Scarborough theatre Company. His cast included Janet Dale, a former county drama advisor in North Devon, later to make her mark at Stratford, notably in 'The Merry Wives of Windsor', and at the National Theatre as the Queen in 'The Madness of George the Third'.

The Plough has had its share of financial crises. In 1989 it was rescued by an anonymous benefactor who helped to clear its debts with a gift of £2,000. Local enthusiasts waded in with a further £1,000. By 1990 Press headlines proclaimed 'The Plough Digs Itself Out of the Red'. Beaford have much more of a direct say in Plough affairs these days, and its arts programmes and those of Beaford have been substantially integrated. The Beaford administration has also found in the Plough a geographically convenient operating base.

9

Student/Adult Theatre at Bideford, North Devon, & Ilfracombe Colleges

The expansion of adult theatre in North Devon has had an impact on the work of drama departments in colleges and schools.

A lead in this direction has been given by the North Devon College in which an arts block contains a theatre with one of the best open stage facilities in the area. It is known as the Blacksell Centre.

Here an exciting repertory has been provided under the leadership, first of Chester Lovering and then of John Marks.

Vigorous activity by the Apprentices student group has been coupled with that of an adult company. Lately the two have combined their efforts.

An offshoot of the student section has been the creation of a drama group called Imago, involving itself particularly with issues of social relevance, such as Aids and child-abuse, dramatised in work taken to schools. The Aids project was frank and explicit, and there was no undue moralising. It was almost always received with genuine rather than polite attention, especially since the age-gap between performers and audience was relatively small. Objections might have been anticipated to such episodes as a demonstration on the fitting of condoms. Such apprehensions, in fact, proved groundless.

Student-adult productions have invariably drawn full houses and occasionally touring professional groups have been brought in. The student contribution has ranged from 'Alice in Wonderland' to

Brecht's 'The Mother' and from O'Casey's 'The Shadow of the Gunman' to 'Toad of Toad Hall'.

A similar expansion of drama has occurred in Bideford and Ilfracombe schools. Bideford College has been equipped with its own 200 seater theatre containing a raked auditorium. Under the leadership of Neil Bennion, the amenity has been made available not only for student productions but for touring professional groups. Before this theatre was created, Bideford had no purpose-built accommodation in which plays could be staged. The then headmaster, John Dare, resolved at the outset that the new venue should be used in the widest sense for the benefit of the town and the district around.

Ilfracombe college also has its own drama studio and this has become the base of Studio theatre, a group whose standards have risen quite spectacularly, under the leadership of Chris Jackson, during recent years.

John Marks has run his Open theatre at Ilfracombe. The work included some interesting experiments. For E A Whitehead's 'The Foursome' each performance was given in the living room of a private house. Marks tackled controversial subjects, such as Robert Patrick's 'Kennedy's Children'. 'The Winter's Tale' was given a Victorian setting. The old morality play 'Everyman' was featured in Pilton's Medieval Fair.

A performance I shall always remember was 'The Killing of Sister George', a sensitive exploration of lesbianism built around the dropping of a well-established character from a T V soap. Joan Homewood and Anne Wright had leading roles.

Open theatre also gave a production of 'King Lear' with Donald McCallam in the title role. Only one other amateur actor in the area has tackled the role of Lear and that was Jack Westcott for The Friends.

I have only witnessed two student portrayals of Hamlet, one by Philip Osment for William Benson's production at Barnstaple Grammar School (Osment later went on to Oxford and became theatre director of Gay Sweatshop, a company which has frequently been in the news) and the other by Michael Stoneham at the North Devon College. Stoneham is now studying for a degree in theatre at Plymouth University. His ambition is to be a teacher but also to associate himself with active participation in stage plays.

REVIEW 1980
(North Devon Journal)

Unacceptable face of Prospero

'The Tempest' –Ilfracombe Open Theatre

Predictably, John Mark's production of 'The Tempest' for Ilfracombe Open Theatre is a director's piece which reflects a thoughtful and in some respects unorthodox reading of the play.

In essence, it is a liberal interpretation, in line with modern progressive ideas.

The point of controversy is the treatment of Prospero, so often cosily depicted as a father-figure. Here it is on the less acceptable face of benevolent dictatorship that stress is laid.

The usurped duke is himself a usurper, the occupying power on someone else's island. Ariel and Caliban are among the natives that he has oppressed.

Calvinistic

It is an emphasis reinforced by the gaunt Prospero of Donald McCallam, a dour Scot whose Becket in 'Murder in the Cathedral' I once likened to John Knox.

Puritanism remains rife within him. His harsh treatment of Caliban is draconian punishment for sexual lust. The fierceness of his concern for Miranda's chastity exceeds the bounds of normal parental care.

He is savage in his attitude to those whom he thinks have wronged him, and forgiveness sticks in his throat.

Moreover, he does not surrender his mastery of the black arts cheerfully. When he breaks his staff and burns his books, he does so with misgivings in his heart.

An intriguing facet is Prospero's relationship with Ariel, whom Jenny Rogers, in a lively performance, makes an essentially feminine sprite. It seems to have an emotional base.

The more traditional romantic element in the story is handled with sensitivity by Leoni Antoniazzi's diffident Miranda and the handsome Ferdinand of Andrew Jones.

Matthew Clement's Caliban, not made to look monstrous, is an intelligent portrayal of what repression can do to the soul.

A robust Stephano by Vincent Boni, supported by Anthony Richard's Trinculo, gives breezy light relief.

Amiable Bore

Keith Denby's Sebastian and Ahlan Davison-Gray's Antonio are dashing villains who show little remorse. Graham Scott-Goldstone's Alonzo stays

39

constantly amazed by what is going on around him and Harold Mayo's Gonzalo is, no less correctly, an amiable bore.

The scenes involving masque and mime, the propless shipwreck, the 'Ban Caliban' business, and the seduction of the rustics all come off well.

If you monkey about with magicians presumably you have to accept the consequences. Retribution has come to John Marks in the form of a slipped disk.

Other actors involved with him in the exercise, to be repeated at Ilfracombe Community College Theatre this week are Susan Cresswell, Tony Jewell, Andrew Little, Gary Mills, Phyllis Jewell, Susanne Brewer, Rosemary Peyton, Linda Welburn, and Alison Todd.

§

REVIEW 1980
(North Devon Journal)

No people like show-people

'Hamlet' – Footsbarn Theatre Company

Purists may feel that the Footsbarn 'Hamlet' is a theatrical misfortune more appropriate to 'Macbeth'.

Not that the company worry overmuch about the reactions of purists. They are always prepared to massacre a text if in so doing they can gain opportunity for invention and visual effect.

Their acting is fast, physical, and exciting. By comparison, it makes ice-hockey seem as ponderous as chess.

Pole-vaulting

The players pole-vault their way onto a small, circular stage. Once there it is a case of every man for himself.

Inevitably, the poetry is the first casualty. Not many of the speeches survive, and those that do are paraphrased freely.

'Above all, be true to yourself,' becomes a substitute for, 'to thine own self be true'. At least it shows what Series Three has done to the authorised version of the Book of Common Prayer.

Briefly one catches a snatch of, 'O that this too too solid flesh would melt.' But it is soon put to silence by competition from a brass band.

The characters, including Hamlet, are bizarre caricatures. The furtive Claudius looks more like Abdul the Damned than any usurper of a Danish throne.

That the Polonius should have made me think of Malcolm Muggeridge is justifiable. But deadlier liberties are taken with Gertrude, portrayed as a commedia dell'arte sex-pot, with pancake white clown make-up and painted-doll rouged cheeks.

Ophelia appears virtually topless in the mad scene, and no-one will grumble about the extent of that disclosure. It is with her, more than any

40

of the others, that one becomes emotionally involved. But Hamlet has a supreme moment of indecision when he resists the temptation to kill his step-father at prayers.

A high old time is had with the ghost episode, which engulfs the auditorium in Elsinore fog. Polonius's death behind the arras - called a curtain - is made the more horrific through a javelin nailing him by the throat.

The strolling thespians at Claudius's court are extrovert tumblers. Much slapstick surrounds the gravediggers. Alas, poor Yorick - he goes out with the cuts.

Extravaganza

Footsbarn Shakespeare is an entertaining business for those who already know the orthodox version. How the author could hope to claim royalties on their current extravaganza is anyone's guess. But as pure theatre, designed to make audiences sit up in their seats and roll about in the aisles, it comes off.

The company are Maggie Watkiss, Dave Johnston, Joey Cunningham, Paddy Hayter, Rod Goodall, Simon Steward-Richardson, Annie Robinson, Margaret Biereye, Warwick Moreton, Chunky Pilley, John Arnott, Dave Hayter, John Kilby, and Shirley Hayter, with Maggie Jones designing props and masks and the dance being directed by Audrey Cook.

§

REVIEW 1981
(North Devon Journal)

Prospero as an island queen

'The Tempest' – Actors Touring Company

Apart from the minor detail of converting Prospero into a woman, ATC's brilliantly inventive treatment of 'The Tempest', presented at the North Devon College on Thursday, was scrupulously faithful to text and plot.

One could only speculate on the motivations behind the choice of Valerie Braddell for the principal role.

But having embarked on his course, John Retallack capitalised where he could.

He brought new sexual overtones into Prospero's relationships with Caliban and Ariel, and these fitted logically enough into the revised context.

Moreover, not even a male chauvinist pig could have faulted Miss Braddell on her handling of the lines.

Christine Bishop's balletic Ariel performed in complete sympathy with the music. This included 'Where the Bee Sucks' arranged in a strikingly original form.

41

Slapstick

Jack Ellis's Caliban was not excessively monstrous, and the timing of his knock-about with Chris Barnes's Trinculo and Raymond Sawyer's bowler-hatted Stephano, behaving like a couple of music-hall comedians, was superb.

At one point, passages from 'Macbeth,' 'Richard the Third,' and 'Hamlet' crept in, and there was even an appearance by the bear from 'The Winter's Tale.'

This was ATC creating the kid of exuberant theatre which it achieved in 'Don Quixote' at the Plough twelve months ago.

Mr Retallack allowed himself further licence. Thus Ariel died on regaining freedom, and the island was rolled up into a neat package of floor-covering as soon as the magic stopped.

One scarcely noticed that the presentation was in modern dress. But Paul Elkins's Ferdinand and Denise Nixon's Miranda were creatures of the mid-20th century.

The former had no trace of romanticism about him - he was the antithesis of the traditional Prince Charming - and the latter was wild, wayward, and rebellious. One sensed that they would have trouble with her once she got back to Milan.

William Russell Enoch presided like a diplomat over the Neapolitan court. Not even the shipwreck could disturb his urbane exterior, for he flicked the experience off his immaculate morning suit. But real tension was created by the assassination attempt.

§

REVIEW 1982
(North Devon Journal)

What eyes don't see...

'Equus'
Ilfracombe Open Theatre, The North Devon College

The role of the stallion in the imagery of sexual fantasy is a theme which various authors and film-makers have explored.

When the young stable lad in Peter Schaffer's 'Equus' takes a metal spike and blinds six horses, therefore, we realise that something vastly deeper than sheer viciousness is involved.

The secrets are buried full fathom five in the boy's subconscious.

The dexterity with which they are brought gradually to the surface is an exercise in detection worthy of Sherlock Holmes.

Slowly there emerges a picture of formative years spent in an atmosphere of domestic tension.

Atheism

Father, is an atheist, an old fashioned Socialist with a WEA inspired reverence for book learning.

He believes that the God-cult, down through history, has been responsible for most of the world's suffering.

What else could be expected, he argues, from a brand of theism which uses as its symbol the image of its deity nailed to a cross and refreshes itself spiritually through the pretence of eating the god's flesh and drinking his blood.

Mother, a schoolteacher who is accredited with having married beneath her, is a devout Christian with a prissy virtue-orientated conception of religious faith.

Their son, not surprisingly, experiences an emotional need to worship which he finds almost impossible to fulfil.

Eventually he settles for paying his homage to horses, partly because of their magnificence as creatures and partly because of the carnal stimulation which he obtains through physical contact as he rides naked on their backs.

There are also darker mysteries in the relationship which he has neither the age nor the knowledge to comprehend.

What his mother has taught him is that the eye of god is all-seeing and that from it there can be no concealment of sinning.

Guilty and humiliated when his first attempt at intercourse with a girl fails, he senses that he has been watched by the divine being. His act of mutilation is a savage and primitive response.

John Mark's production deliberately stripped a highly theatrical play of all the trappings of its theatricality.

The mood was as clinical as the atmosphere of the consulting room in which most of the action was set, and it was in this cool detachment that the strength of Open Theatre's performance lay.

The approach was reflected faithfully in Graham Scott-Goldstone's psychiatrist who in probing the motivations of his patients is brought face to face with the impotence and inadequacy within himself.

Passion

The actor's one major weakness was technical; a tendency to swallow final syllables.

But there was a tense interaction between him and Paul Fullarton's boy, smouldering aggressively with suppressed passion and power.

Bob Edwards and Daphne Lock made out a good case for the parents - every part needs to be played from its own viewpoint - and Su Scott-Goldstone's magistrate had a quality of diction which set a standard for the group.

Carol Altass portrayed the girl who attempts the seduction and Marge Pearce the nurse. The horses, beautifully stylised with headpieces fashioned by Richard Challacombe and Joan Homewood, were represented by Brian Pearce and Ahlan Davison-Gray.

43

§

REVIEW 1982
(North Devon Journal)

Timing it right

'Mother Courage' – Open Theatre, Ilfracombe Community College

As the Falklands euphoria continues, Ilfracombe Open Theatre have been touring North Devon with what is probably the most savage play ever written in the cause of peace.

Bertold Brecht's 'Mother Courage', is set against the background of the mid-European conflict of the 1600s, after the revolt of Bohemia against the rule of the Hapsburgs.

It was a Protestant-Catholic quarrel which lasted over a period of thirty years.

Squalid living

Brecht's anti-heroine, who gives her name to the title, is a camp-follower who has battened on to the situation, a small-time trader who makes a squalid living out of human misery.

She becomes so involved in her life-style that she cannot break with it even though it costs her a daughter and several sons.

The message is that in the long term no-one can hope to benefit from the war, the target of the attack being the international arms-dealers who do their best to defy this natural law.

An unforeseen irony was that the production should have reached performance just at a time when the public in Britain were beginning to ask whether it was true that NATO-made weapons sold to the Fascist junta in Argentina had been used against British Task Force troops.

John Marks's production pointed up the bitterness in the writing, achieving it particularly in the harshness of the delivery of the songs.

War was portrayed as a gross obscenity, unrelieved by the valour sometimes involved in it, and made more offensive when endorsed by the Christian church.

Mary Brighten's Courage was fierce, tough, earthy, and physically filthy down to the tips of her finger-nails.

A brash Northcountry accent fitted perfectly to round off as sound a characterisation as we are likely to see in amateur drama this year.

The robust humour seemed somewhat muted but the Brecht weakness of disrupting continuity by episodic construction was substantially overcome.

The plot flowed smoothly, although possibly at a more intellectual level than the author, who wrote primarily for peasants, would have wished.

It was essentially an ensemble piece, although one can scarcely bury in anonymity the pathos of Hannah Goodyear's dumb Kattrin, the hypocrisy in Andy Penman's lewd and worldly chaplain, or the gaudy wanton created in Marge Pearce's Yvette.

Double-hate

The male roles - notably Paul Fullerton's Eilif, Robert Lord's recruiting officer (Brecht hated the military almost as much as he hated Christians), Graham Scott-Goldstone's sergeant, Richard Challacombe's cook, and Donald McCallam's authoritative storyteller - were all well done.

The other players were Robin Emery, John Baxter, John Humphreys, Mary Prince, and Daphne Lock, with music by Kim McGavin, Mathew Arnold, and Elizabeth White, and lighting by Sophie Speller and Gavin Jones.

Politically Brecht was a communist. It is fair to add that his views on militarism would be as unpopular in the Kremlin as in No 10 Downing Street at the present time.

§

REVIEW 1984
(North Devon Journal)

Alice on the rock

'Alice in Wonderland' – Apprentice Student Theatre Group

John Marks, director of the Apprentices Student Theatre Group, is not the first reader of children's literature to regard 'Alice in Wonderland' as a strange and disturbing book.

The degree of disturbance was scarcely mitigated in his adaptation for Apprentices Student theatre.

It was a noisy and robust treatment in what might be broadly categorised as the rock idiom.

Songs were arranged by Keith Nixon Kerslake and incidental music was added by a group consisting of Duncan Bachell, Alex and Carol Duncan, Frazer Osment, and Michael Walsh.

Lyrics drowned

They played their own compositions from the gallery. The lyrics were witty but sheer volume frequently drowned words.

The dramatisation portrayed Alice as a lonely and isolated child, trying desperately to come to terms with the adult environment around her.

To reinforce the point, Carroll's characters, down to the White Rabbit, the Cheshire Cat, and the March Hare, retained human form and the performance was costumed in a trendy style of modern dress.

Shantelle Way's Alice, looking as demure as a Tenniel illustration, embodied a correct element of Brechtian alienation; she observed without allowing herself to become emotionally involved.

Cassandra Clyde's Queen combined the physique of Marie Lloyd with the formidability of Margaret Thatcher, a blending of terrifying proportions. Colourful roles included Patrick Furse's alcoholic king, Michelle Diwell's hep-caterpillar, Trevor Ellis's Cheshire feline, speaking through his teeth with an officers' mess accent, David Marochan's campish executioner, Pewter White's Mad Hatter, Haydn Davies's March Hare, and the mock turtle of Ryk Smith.

Insinuating duchess

Joanne Walker insinuated her way through the duchess with a possessiveness which at times seemed morally suspect. Charmion Falkner contributed a gem of a Cockney Gryphon, and Claire Humphrey made a down-to-earth comic of the cook.

David Lavalette was the White Rabbit, and others in the team were Tracy Short, Stephanie Chichester, Isabelle Czekajio, Sarah Thompson, Rosemary Chichester, Melani Widders, Katherine Roff, Clive Andrews, Christopher Dearle, Patrick Combes, James Parker, and Maxine Vowles. The pianist was Nicole Cartlidge, the stage manager was Tony Goodwin, and lighting was handled by Ian Gred.

§

REVIEW 1985
(North Devon Journal)

Night of the leeks

'Under Milk Wood' – Arts Theatre Company,
New Theatre, North Devon College

Among ex-patriate Welshmen national pride is a characteristic which dies hard.

It is not only on St David's Day that they honour the achievements of such notable kinsmen as, for example, J P R Williams, Owen Glendower and David Lloyd-George.

It may surprise some people to know that Chester Lovering, co-director of the Arts theatre Company and head of drama at the North Devon College, is a son of the Principality.

For voices

This being so, it follows that one of his thespianic ambitions should have been to produce Dylan Thomas's 'Under Milk Wood' in the manner in which it was originally intended to be heard.

It was written as 'a play for voices' tailored primarily for steam radio.

And behind the choice of medium there was sound reasoning; such personalities as No-Good Boyo, Capt. Cat, Organ Morgan and the Dai

46

Breads are better imagined than seen.

It is also a piece orchestrated for pure Welsh intonations. And the cast in this performance in the New Theatre of the North Devon College was drawn exclusively from local residents who have originated from Wales.

They were able to communicate naturally the lyrical poetry in Thomas's panorama of life in a Welsh village.

It was an observation which made the author less than universally popular among his own countrymen.

His impression of bethel-dominated hypocrisy came too near truth for comfort.

But in this interpretation it was seen to be no more than a jest, neither satirical nor malicious, but delivered with affection and warmth.

There is nothing quite so good-humoured as making fun of the idiosyncrasies in one's own family, especially when the comment is valid.

And to chaff at his own folk, his basic regard for them not being called into question, was Thomas's clear intention here.

There remains little doubt that his personal sympathies lay more with Polly Garter dreaming of her love-making with the deceased Willie Wee as she goes about her business as parish trollop, than with Mrs Ogmore-Pritchard, telling her husband to 'polish the potatoes' and demanding that 'before you let the sun in, mind it wipes its shoes.'

Legitimate prejudice

But prejudices are legitimate, even when incorporated in family jokes.

The director was himself a member of the cast. Others were June Davies, Irene McLoughlan, Pam Mackey, David Davies, Ceri Evans, Roger Greening, Tony McLoughlin, Colin Skene and Mary Row.

Together they generated a mood splendidly furtive. The Polly Garter ballad was sung with sensitivity by Sandra Squires, married to a Welshman, but the only English member of the team.

§

REVIEW 1989
(North Devon Journal)

Madhouse epic

Marat-Sade – North Devon College

Revolution is the theme of Peter Weiss's Brechtian-style epic, generally known as 'The Marat-Sade'. It is a play within a play, ostensibly performed as a therapeutic exercise by the inmates of a lunatic asylum.

Perhaps wisely, John Marks preferred to recruit his company from Open Theatre and Apprentices, the North Devon College adult and student drama groups.

Behind bars

They acted behind bars, which wobbled occasionally, thus creating apprehension that the structure might collapse, letting the thespians loose on their audience. Happily such a disaster was avoided, but it was all rather like visiting Bedlam for a Sunday treat.

The argument in the plot centred around whether revolution ever achieves its purpose and whether liberty, equality and fraternity are really no more than impractical ideals.

The case for this assumption was put by Colin Mackey's coldly aloof de Sade, confident in the logic of his own reasoning. He believed realistically that the world belongs to the individualist and thereafter it is a law of nature that the weakest should go to the wall.

His adversary in the debate was Michael Stoneham's eczema-tortured Marat, a zealot convinced that the old order of privilege must be stamped out – by mass executions if necessary – to make way for a brave new world.

What could have become an exercise in dialectics was saved from this fate by the inventiveness of the direction.

Violence simmered under the surface. The lunatics rumbled like threatening volcanoes. When the eruption finally came it was a sight terrifying and magnificent to behold.

Vicky Hemmingway's Corday, the girl who knifes Marat in his bath, was, like many assassins, the manipulated zombie, virtually programmed for her mission.

Steve Cox and Michael Magnet served admirably as heralds and a chorus of four girls symbolised the mob.

Ensemble

This was ensemble theatre in the full sense, the team containing Tanya Elliott, Neil Rudd, Chris Jewell, Tim Coles, David Pratt, Sarah Baxter, Becky Jeffrey, Richard Smith, Paula Morante, Caroline Berridge, Andrew Barker, Peter Bird, Amy Charles, Peter Godfrey, Fay Hughes, Norman James, Emma Macey Withey, Lynn Rabbett, Andy Davies, Kirsten Horner, Su Scott Goldstone, Yvonne Spooner and David Wise.

The musicians were Jason Gooze, Andrew Murray and Howard Thomas. Tony Goodwin and David Baker designed the set.

§

A bedtime story

Frankie and Johnny – Open Theatre

Neither Mary Whitehouse nor Barbara Cartland could be relied on to nominate Terence McNally's 'Frankie and Johnny in the Claire de Lune' for an Olivier award.

There are only two characters, a waitress who has been battered by a previous lover and a male cook, with a high school background and a respect for Shakespeare, who has been gaoled for fraud.

Paula Morante's production for Open Theatre at the North Devon College had the distinction of being the first of this play in Britain to be presented by an amateur cast.

Rightly, she refused to bowdlerise the content, the most explicit that has been staged in the area for many months. She merely advised those likely to be offended, more especially by the language, to stay home.

Analysis

The setting is Manhattan and the action begins in darkness; sounds suggest that a couple, sharing a bed, are heavily involved in making love.

It is a practice in which they indulge, or threaten to indulge, at intervals as the plot unfolds.

Between bouts, they analyse their performance, the physical attributes of each other and the barriers to a permanent relationship between them.

One of these is cultural, the girl's education being somewhat inferior to the man's, with the result that she regards his vocabulary with mistrust. Yet, after their own fashion, they are romantics at heart and neither has fully matured.

Sensitivity

Michael Stoneham, tall, lean and patronising, and Kathie Richards, shorter, well-rounded and apprehensive, created a mood of sensitivity and maintained a certain rhythm in their lines. Their duologue was admirably sustained over a period of nearly two hours.

A simple set helped to create atmosphere, the only props being a television set, a cooking stove (the girl's appetite for food was almost as insatiable as the man's for sex) and, of course, the bed.

The stage manager was Norman James

§

Erupting on to the stage

Volcano Theatre – Blacksell Centre, Barnstaple

After their own fashion Volcano theatre have been paying a tribute to William Shakespeare, visiting the Blacksell Centre at Barnstaple with a production which they have called 'L.O.V.E.'.

The Bard's contribution to this celebration was to provide the best part of the script.

But this was no mere reading of his sonnets – the concentration was powerfully and evocatively on the movement.

Sex, after all, is primarily a physical activity, hardly to be commemorated solely in a recital of words.

The verse, some of the finest ever penned in the English language, provided little more than an accompaniment to activity of a more athletic kind.

Magnificent

Much of it was spent squirming on the floor and occasionally transferring itself to a magnificent scarlet-sheeted four-poster bed.

Acknowledging the probability that Shakespeare was bi-sexual – the sonnets, after all, were dedicated to a man – Paul Davies and Liam Steele made erotic play for and with each other, but frequently turned their amorous attentions to the third member of the company, Fern Smith.

Her purpose may well have been to represent the Dark Lady, Shakespeare's mistress whose identity, if she ever existed, has never been established.

She was depicted as a predatory seductress of formidable proportions and jealous with it. In her enjoyment of sexual fulfilment, viciousness and violence were integral parts.

Miss Smith, a vigorous actress, dominated much of the action. Her interpretation of women's rights was that, if wild oats were to be sown, it was her privilege to harvest the crop.

The director, Nigel Charnock, in a programme note, thanks 'Mr Shakespeare' for allowing him to take 'indecent liberties with the text'.

As an observer, I found the experience quite liberating. I was reminded that in my early days as a critic, the Lord Chamberlain would have vetoed much of the material.

We have progressed somewhat in 40 years. At the same time it must be conceded that sex, as a recreation, can hardly be regarded like soccer as a spectator sport.

What was encouraging was the size of the audience, which reached capacity proportions with an average age of around 25. This must have gratified the Beaford Centre, who promoted the event.

Volcano describe themselves a 'A new generation of performers, committed to movement and meaning'. Thus they reject formal scripts.

Explosive

It was not the company's first visit to North Devon. They performed 'Medea: Sex Wars' (the sources including 'The Scum Manifesto,' written by the anarcho-feminist, Valerie Solanis, said to have inaugurated a movement for 'cutting up men' in 1991).

Volcano is an explosive unit, which has no inhibitions about living up to its title. Long may it continue to receive Arts Council, Welsh Arts Council and British Council support.

It also works for Crusaid, a charity dedicated to the helping of people suffering from the effects of AIDS and HIV.

§

10

The Importance of Schools Theatre

Schools, private and state, have contributed massively to the expansion of theatrical activity in North Devon. In the state sector, Edward Blacksell, at Barnstaple Boys' Secondary Modern School, instituted an annual Shakespearean production, thereby refuting the fallacy that the so-called '11-plus failures' could not undertake performances at that level. (One detractor had called it 'casting pearls before swine').

At Barnstaple Grammar School, Jack Westcott and Dai Williams established a reputation for high comedy. When William Benson took over the direction he achieved successes with 'Hamlet', 'The Fire Raisers' and 'The Crucible'. Robert Barber, with a cast numbering 80, followed up with 'The Caucasian Chalk Circle' and a 'Robin Hood' which was boldly realistic, resisting any of the 'riding through the glen' attitude.

At Ilfracombe School, John Marks staged the most imaginative and caustic interpretation of 'Oh, What a Lovely War' that I have experienced. Even his headmaster had apprehensions about the reaction of the local Establishment to its treatment of the reputation of Haig. Later Chris Jackson presented a highly atmospheric 'Macbeth' with Neil Prideaux in the title role and Catherine Eschele as his notorious spouse.

The school drama group was later merged into Studio Theatre, with notable revivals of 'She Stoops to Conquer' (Emma Mountcastle as a charming Kate and Doreen Reading as the socially ambitious wife of the country squire) and 'The Entertainer' in which Larry Fabian exceeded all expectations as Archie Rice.

Bideford Grammar School had already achieved a lively reputation, especially through the work of Robert Clyde, Geoff Abbot, and Bob Terrell, who in Obey's 'Noah' had the central character quietly singing 'A Life On The Ocean Waves' as he built the ark.

When the school went comprehensive and acquired its own theatre it became known as Bideford College. Neil Bennion, from Exmouth Comprehensive, was appointed to direct its activities. His musicals have included, 'Fiddler On The Roof', 'Matchgirls', 'West Side Story', 'Guys and Dolls', 'Oliver', and in my view the best of the series, 'Cabaret', with Emma Brimacombe and Samantha Barrett sharing the role (on alternate nights) of Sally Bowles. On the straight side, John Hodgson's 'Twelfth Night' in 1991 was the first Shakespeare play to be undertaken by the school for twenty years.

Braunton School drama has flourished under the leadership of Janet Cotter (formerly a producer with The Friends as Janet Potter). She has never been afraid to tackle controversial subjects. 'The Rotten Side Of The Apple' was a searing indictment of social malpractices in the United States. Her 'Flowers Never Fade', based on rural bigotry, received strong commendation in a National Theatre assessment. The students researched it and wrote the text.

In what might be termed the private sector, West Buckland School has a record for theatre dating back to the headmastership of the Reverend Ernest Harries, who was a fan of Gilbert and Sullivan. In the 1970s there was a colourful period of activity under the leadership of Ralph Pearce, who succeeded me as chairman of North Devon Drama Federation. One day he invited me to accompany him to Instow, where his senior students were presenting 'a pop oratorio' written by a pair that no-one had heard of. His intimation that it might have a future turned out to be prophetic. The piece was 'Joseph And The Amazing Technicolour Dreamcoat' by Andrew Lloyd Webber and Tim Rice.

West Buckland has the distinction of being the first North Devon school to support Globelink, the Sam Wannamaker project to recreate the Elizabethan Globe Theatre, where most of Shakespeare's plays had their first performances. When West Buckland launched a £660,000 appeal to convert a school house for boarders into an arts complex, including a drama studio, Sam's daughter Zoe, herself an actress of national repute, became one of the patrons.

Shebbear College has achieved an equally distinguished record for drama. Ashley Williams has handled the musicals and the 'legiti-mate' side has had among its directors John Shaw, Greg Warren, R H West and Ged Kennedy, who in 1993 staged a modern dress version of Moliere's 'La Malade Imaginaire'. I had a special interest in the Moliere since at my own school the head of English was even more ambitious, chosing to present it in the native French. Hardly any of us (certainly not me) had any clear understanding of the language. Fortunately for us, the audience hadn't either. When we dried, we improvised with such stock text book phrases as 'la plume de ma tante est dans la salle-à-manger'. No-one among our patrons was any the wiser!

An auspicious Shebbear production, by the headmaster, George Kingsnorth, was 'King Henry The Fifth', staged in 1980. A year later I sat next to him to witness an hilarious production by Brian Watson of N F Simpson's 'One Way Pendulum'. The hero of the play is a young man obsessed with the idea of training 500 speak-your-weight machines to perform Handel's 'Messiah'. The humour left the head-master completely bewildered. I don't think Theatre of the Absurd was really his scene.

Since Shebbear was exclusively a boys' school, Edgehill College (exclusively girls) sent volunteers to play the feminine roles in Shebbear productions. This offered welcome opportunities for romantic assignations but Edgehill has done highly satisfactory work on its own account, as with the Ted Hughes nativity play 'The Coming Of the Kings', 'A Comedy of Errors', 'The Tempest', and, more recently Charlotte Keatley's 'My Mother Said I Never Should', a study of mother-and daughter relationships across the period of a century, which was taken to the Plough. In Christine Roy's produc-tion of a nativity play in 1978 the plot was set in a Britain with the National Front in power and Joseph depicted as a West Indian. The producer resisted strongly assertions that it was a Marxist exercise.

The drama group at Edgehill is now known as On The Edge.

Edgehill girls have also featured in Grenville College productions, joining forces for such pieces as 'Iolanthe', 'HMS Pinafore', 'Trial By Jury', and 'The Importance of Being Earnest'. 'Trial by Jury' in 1975 celebrated the centenary of the Gilbert and Sullivan partnership and was set in the Gatsby period. 'The Government Inspector', directed by Tony Paris, was the first production to be staged in a new school hall. For 'Patience' in 1992 the feminine roles were taken by the Stella Maris School. These two schools combined again in 'She Stoops To Conquer' a year later.

11

The Work of North Devon Dancing Schools

The revue side of North Devon theatre over the years has been provided mainly by the Ilfracombe Dancing schools of Betty Blackmore and Esmé Preston, who also staged an annual pantomime. More recently it has involved the Daystar School of Dance, run by Joan Spear and Teresa Crossman and Kathy Wellington's Pilton School of Dance.

Betty Blackmore, a former Tiller Girl, has been a local dance school principal for about forty years. In 1992 she was honoured by a tribute in the style of 'This Is Your Life'. Sadly it marked the last public appearance of Ada Buckingham, for years the dame in Esmé Preston's pantomimes. She died only a few days later.

The Preston record of local productions spanned fifty-one years. Neither the second world war nor cancer dampened her determination to keep her show on the road. Her first production was presented in 1930 soon after she moved from South Wales to Ilfracombe. As a trainer of dancers, she had a formidable record as a disciplinarian. She tended to treat theatre critics in the same way.

After I had reviewed her pantomimes, for which her daughter, Sandra Paxford was script-writer, she invariably telephoned me on the morning of publication to remind me that I was an ignoramus so far as dance shows were concerned. A few days later she could call at my office and invite me out for coffee. If ours was a bizarre love-hate relationship, it was founded on a strange kind of mutual respect. The Preston reputation was known nationally. When Marie Rambert brought her ballet to Barnstaple, one of the questions she asked me was whether I knew 'that remarkably accomplished dance teacher at

Ilfracombe'. A record of Preston successes supports this assessment. Philip Broomhead, one of her pupils, made his mark with the royal Ballet. Charles Ley went on to join the International Ballet and became the Swedish state ballet master. Shirley Brett joined the Clarkson Rose company, the professional tours of the Dobie Twins have already been mentioned, Lindsay Rowe-Roberts, Pauline Lane and Joachim Chandler went on from her tuition to follow stage careers.

When Esmé Preston died many people felt that they had suffered a personal loss.

A third presenter of revue-style entertainment in Ilfracombe has been Pauline Heawood who ran Ilfracombe Minstrels and later ATT (All Things Theatrical). The Minstrels followed the pattern of the television series, The Black and White Minstrels, whose musical director, George Mitchell, was stationed at Ilfracombe with the Royal Army Pay Corps during the second world war. Another celebrity at Ilfracombe during the early war years was CoCo the Clown, who was serving with the Pioneer Corps.

§

REVIEW 1953
(North Devon Journal)

Puss in Boots

Portland Dance Academy

Anita Dobie, who played Rollo in Esmé Preston's 'Puss in Boots' at Ilfracombe on Thursday is a singularly well-equipped principal boy. Over and above the physical attributes, she has a clear voice and an engaging stage manner, all of which she has developed substantially since she played the lead in 'Miss Muffet' twelve months ago.

Not that this was exclusively Miss Dobie's triumph. There was an equally polished performance by Valerie Hewitt, a girl with a clear understanding of the spirit of pantomime, who rose completely to the task of making the cat the real hero of the piece. Immaculate costuming and some good sets laid the foundation of a production that was not lacking in colour, and although the three and a half hour run could have been pruned with advantage by at least 30 thirty minutes, it was, by and large, a more even performance by the company than last year's.

There was some particularly graceful work by Diana Battrick. Songs that appealed were 'There She Goes', performed with sparkle by Penelope Dobie, Wendy Pile, and Diana Battrick and Miss Hewitt's two duets. 'Carols And Crosses' with Dennis Ground as the giant, and 'You're Just In

Love', with the principal boy.

More was made of the comedy than is usual in these pantomimes, thanks mainly to the individualistic Sandra and the slapstick humour of Brian Wilson and Betty Bennington, who gave us the novelty of a pseudo-academic dame. Gillian Latham, though apparently no singer, made a graceful and attractive principal girl.

§

12

The Barnstaple Operatic Society

So far, I have said little about amateur theatre which has kept North Devon drama alive during several of its lean periods.

One of the longest established amateur groups in North Devon is Barnstaple Operatic Society. It was founded in 1900 although initially it had a chequered career.

Its production of 'Iolanthe' in 1906 clashed with a general election. Despite the fact that the opera has strong political associations, the production incurred a financial loss.

A revival came in 1920, being instigated by J H L Brewer, then town clerk of Barnstaple, Sydney Harper, Jack Brannam, and H Garfield Pearce.

I have already mentioned my encounter at the age of seven with 'The Yeomen of the Guard'. A couple of years later I saw the company again in 'The Mikado', and marvelled at the pomposity of John Brewer's Poo-Bah and the impish humour of Tom Knill's Ko-Ko. I knew the latter slightly since he called at our house about twice a year to tune my mother's piano. A decade or so later his charming and attractive daughter, Pamela, became a colleague, the first woman journalist with whom I worked.

The society stuck rigidly to the Gilbert and Sullivan repertoire and had a formidable director in Clara Dow. She had been a principal in productions directed by Sir William Gilbert. To call her a traditionalist would be a masterpiece of understatement. Every minor move on stage had to follow precisely the pattern that Gilbert had laid down.

I never counted Miss Dow as a member of my fan club. I infuriated her by suggesting in print that the society, having played Gilbert and Sullivan to a point of exhaustion, should try something else. She reacted as an Islamic Fundamentalist might to 'The Satanic Verses', denouncing such heresy in a curtain speech.

Nevertheless the Society eventually decided to include work other than the Savoy operas in their repertoire. It was decision dictated by market forces, only about three of the pieces ('The Gondoliers', 'The Mikado' and 'The Pirates of Penzance') continuing to bring in the crowd.

The break came in the early 1960s and it brought together a highly popular stage partnership between Chester Lovering and Sandra Squires. I class Miss Squires, with Eileen Candy and Mary Chant as one of the three most accomplished female soloists that I have heard on the local amateur stage.

The break was made with 'Rose Marie' and the subsequent run of shows included 'The King and I', 'The Merry Widow', 'Die Fledermaus', 'Waltzes from Vienna', 'The Desert Song' and 'The Vagabond King'. New principals came to the fore, these including Richard Baron, Phyllis Leading, Beryl Behan, and John Down.

The company had its financial setbacks in the 1970s. 'The New Moon' lost £187 and 'The Count of Luxembourg' had a deficit of £456. More cheerful news was that 'Show Boat' had a credit balance of 20 pence, although 'invisible earnings' raised the amount to around £50. 'The Sound of Music' did even better, netting £532. Leads in these shows included Pat Porter, Stan Forrester, Everard Howard, Diane Bosence, John Molland, Mary Trapnell, Jack Blackmore, Michael Davey, Tony Harrington, and Jane Bryan, and the Lovering-Squires partnership was renewed.

The 1980s brought in Paul Greensmith, Tom Stirzaker, Margaret Taylor, John Newton, Carol Blight and Ian Henderson-Begg. Moreover, the Savoy piece were restored to favour, notably in a production by John Down of 'The Yeomen of the Guard'.

An event of the 1990s was the début of Diane Bosence as a producer. Gil Taylor continued in his role of musical director and under his leadership the musical quality of performances have vastly improved. It must break his heart when audiences chatter noisily through overtures evidently not considering them to be part of a performance. Miss Bosence learnt her job as a performer the hard way, for as a small child she had figured in shows by Esmè Preston's dancing school. Her handling of an adult cast revealed the sense of discipline that this experience had inculculated. Her first production, 'The Pirates of Penzance' made a profit of £4,683.

§

REVIEW 1971
(North Devon Journal)

Warm story of faith and love

'The Sound of Music' – Barnstaple Operatic Society

It is a paradox that in the present Pagan age, 'The Sound of Music,' a religious musical play should be attended by almost unlimited box-office success.

The show may be classified as religious theatre, not merely because it has a chorus of nuns and scenes set in a convent. The spirituality goes deeper than that for the very basis on which the story is founded is the acceptance with faith of the Divine Will.

It is this acceptance which takes the young postulant Maria from Nonnberg Abbey to the family of the widower Von Trapp. The love which develops between them sees the Divine purpose fulfilled. And it is faith which enables the Von Trapps to withstand and later to escape from the evil of the Third Reich.

The noted film version was spoiled for me by sentimentality. Mavis Ward's production for Barnstaple Operatic Society substantially avoids this danger, while still permitting emotion to be felt.

The individual performance which does most to dispel mawkishness is Pat Porter's, as the Mother Abbess. Bathos might have been expected to intrude here, Miss Porter, with serene dignity, keeps it at bay.

Giving Maria

Diane Bosence's Maria is played with a generous measure of sincerity which compensates for her limitations as a singer. What is suggested most gratifyingly is Maria's giving nature, the infinite capacity of the girl to offer her love.

This is revealed especially in her dealings with the Von Trapp children, whose affection is seen to be won through sheer goodness of heart.

Looking more Latin than Teutonic, John Chilcott's Von Trapp has the degree of elegance that one expects from this actor. Discomfitted somewhat by Von Trapp the disciplinarian, he develops the character later with quiet strength.

Supporting contributions come from Wendy Morrall, as superficial Elsa and John Molland, as the devotee of expediency, Max Detweller, Jennifer Mock gives Liesl a Germanic flavour and the social uncertainty which besets every girl in her middle-teens.

The best scenes are those in the abbey, where the voices of Miss Porter, Beryl Behan and Ruth Brock add much. I doubt whether any musical staged in Barnstaple since the war has opened on a more impressive note.

Generally, there is limited work for the chorus, and it is all too evident that its male members are of a higher age-group than the girls.

Other parts are played by Gertrude Cresswell, William Hodges, Vera Ford, Carol Blight (doubling Liesl), Jennifer Mock, Peter Woodhams, Roger Ireland, Joan Sanders, Auriol Hayhow, John Skinner, Gillian Dart, and Graham Sergent. The musical director is Martin Wall.

§

REVIEW 1982
(North Devon Journal)

A Sound to make sweet music

'The Sound of Music' – Barnstaple Operatic Society

One sound likely to make music for Barnstaple Operatic Society at the Queen's Hall this week is that of cash ringing up on box-office tills.

Commercial success, of course, is no criterion on which to assess merit in theatre. But at a time when it costs about £6,000 to get a musical on stage even for an amateur production, it is a consideration which no unsubsidised company can afford to overlook.

The show, set in the Austria of the late 1930s, has suffered somewhat from over-exposure. This is the second live performance seen in North Devon since November and the film version was televised at Christmas.

Patrons nevertheless continue to respond to its wholesome romanticism, and in John Down the group has a director well able to inject freshness into a time-worn story. One remembers what he did with 'Fledermaus' at South Molton a few years ago.

Here he has the advantage of a purposeful Maria in Kathy Wellington, not an especially powerful singer nor entirely convincing as the high-spirited novice, but able to grow into the character as it matures.

She possesses a firm line of jaw to suggest determination. In her battle of wills with Von Trapp over the bringing up of his children there is never reason to doubt the result.

Paul Greensmith's bald and bearded Von Trapp has the suave authority of an aristocrat and convinces particularly when required to be emotionally withdrawn

The smooth charm of Tony Harrington's Max can be a scene stealer and one of the most sharply drawn portrayals is Jeremy Mosdell's young Nazi. With Judith Akerman's Liesl he handles delicately the expression of first-love and physically, he looks precisely what Hitler would have wanted from male youth.

Diane Bosence, less than ideally cast as Elsa, has the experience to get something from the role. The convent sisters - Susan Pettifer, Evelyn Phillips, and Janet Norman - sing well, as do the chorus, and Margaret

Taylor's Mother Superior is capable of spectacular top notes.

The children – Ben Greensmith, Michelle le Masurier, Glen Davey, Stephanie Chichester, Charlotte Hart , and Claire Symons – play up enthusiastically.

Gil Taylor is musical director and other principals are John Newton, Janice Gidman, Julia Watchus, Tom Maddern, Jack Blackmore, Joan Symons, and Graham Bailey.

The second team of children are James and Tracey Evans, Anna Hewitt, Marion Loveridge, Melanie Dallyn, and Pierron Lowe.

§

REVIEW 1984
(North Devon Journal)

Gilbert's Eastern promise

'The Mikado' – Barnstaple Operatic Society

Nationally and locally, 'The Mikado' is enjoying a winter of revival.

In London it is the current fare at the Old Vic, and Barnstaple Operatic Society's version at the Queen's Hall this week is the second seen in North Devon within the space of three months.

Because of its location, Laurie Beattie's production needs to make a more spectacular visual impact than did the refreshingly intimate performance at Combe Martin just before Christmas.

Its qualities include the powerfully vocal contribution of a somewhat static chorus, the singing of the romantic leads, and the characterisation in Tony Harrington's Ko-Ko and Richard Wheeler's Poo-Bah.

Poo-Bah is the archetypal bureaucrat for the worship of whom civic centres were erected as temples. Capturing precisely his overblown sense of self-importance, Mr Wheeler (one presumes heavily padded), invests him with a walk which is a cross between a waddle and a strut.

Bouncy Ko-Ko

Mr Harrington, round and bouncy, makes Ko-Ko not only younger than is customary but also measurably more human. He is the little man, conscious of his own limitations and desperately trying to live with the knowledge that he is not up to his job.

Paul Greensmith's Nanki-Poo is essentially a patrician and has the diction to match. Mary Chant's Yum-Yum will be remembered particularly for 'The Sun, Whose Rays', and she is well complemented by Diane Bosence's pertish Pitti-Sing and Janet Norman's less sanguine Peep-Bo.

The sado-comedy of the second act has Tom Maddern as a lofty Mikado and Mary Trapnell as a suitably mock-tragic Katisha. John Newton does what is required of Pish-Tush.

The lighting was, for me, a disappointment, but what has improved immensely in all musicals during recent years is the standard of the orchestral accompaniment. The director here is Gil Taylor and there is an unusually good oboe.

Mr Beattie, following (perhaps unbeknowingly) an example set a couple of years ago by John Down, keeps the curtains open during the overture.

He has no action taking place at this time, but the mere sight of the scenery deters the audience from twittering among itself.

13

The Barnstaple
Musical Comedy Society

A friendly rivalry has always existed between Barnstaple Operatic Society and Barnstaple Musical Comedy Society. It needs to be friendly because the two groups tend to share casts.

Before my time as a critic, the Musical Comedy Society had established a firm following, particularly through the comic roles portrayed by Gwen Killard-Leavey and Bruce Oliver. My first acquaintance with its work was in a production of 'The Arcadians' at the Regal cinema. It was followed by such shows as 'The Lilac Domino', 'The Quaker Girl', and 'The Belle of New York'. They were not all that much to my taste, as they seemed to be devoid of plot, although one could appreciate the spontaneity in such partnerships as those between Charles Dart, the manager of a local bank, and Jimmy Fry.

A major change of direction came in the mid 1950s when the modern vogue of American-style musicals was introduced. The series began with 'Oklahoma' to be followed promptly by 'Annie Get Your Gun', 'Call Me Madam' and 'The Pyjama Game'. In these productions Jill Hatton gave performances that could only be described as tours de force.

The Lovering-Squires partnership was also evident in the Musical Comedy Society's repertoire, most notably in 'Guys and Dolls'.

There followed a long and happy association between the Society and the Lancashire director, Stanley Collins. Repeated visits each autumn won him many friends in the town. He brought in Kathy Hamilton for 'My Fair Lady', Jane Bryan for 'Brigadoon', Pat Porter

65

for 'Hello Dolly', Cilla Harrison for a revival of 'Calamity Jane' and Marion Scotting for 'Half a Sixpence'. His association with North Devon was ended only by the illness which resulted in his death.

Collins produced about 20 shows for the Society and two actresses of considerable potential recruited by him were Maria Aston, whose father, Bob Aston, had played many character roles for the group and Jane Tate.

Miss Aston was to blossom later in 'Annie Get Your Gun'. Her Annie Oakley in 1983 marked the diamond jubilee of the group.

The Society's productions in the early 1990s were directed by Rose Todd, a professional producer from the Midlands who had first come to North Devon to direct 'South Pacific'. She liked the area so much that she decided to make it her home. In 1991 she revived 'Oklahoma', with Alan Bailey as Curly, Jo Dunkley as Laurie, and Lynda McLaughlin as Ado Annie. It made a profit of £4,555. Her 1992 production was 'Hello Dolly' with Vivien Wakefield in the title role. The reconstruction of the Queen's Hall disrupted the Society's activities. They were revived in 1994, Chester Lovering returning to work with the group as director of 'Calamity Jane' in which Jo Wood had the lead.

Family tradition has frequently been evident in local amateur productions as was the case with the Astons, father and daughter. Harry Challacombe had a lead in 'Call Me Madam'; his son Geoffrey played Leopold in 'White Horse Inn' and Rudi in 'The Dancing Years' for Barnstaple Operatic Society. Similarly Lynda McLaughlin's daughter, Rebecca, has been a leading light in Imago at the North Devon College.

Lately the Musical Comedy Society have started a junior section which already promises to provide them with leads for the future years.

§

Jill Hatton plays Ethel Merman's role

'Annie Get Your Gun' – Barnstaple Musical Comedy Society

Irving Berlin's 'Annie Get Your Gun' is the most warm-hearted musical show that I have seen since the war.

Critics seldom agree, but I rate it above 'Oklahoma', that pseudo-folk opera which the Barnstaple society presented last November. It is infinitely more convivial and far less pretentious, but it bases it appeal not so much on its music and the quality of its humour as on the overall spirit of bustle and boisterous fun.

Fortunately, Edward Royce has been able to persuade his company – or nearly all of it – to let their hair down. He has plenty of young talent to play with, and the note of lively abandon that he finds for the first scene is a very practical method of breaking the ice.

And no one responds more readily to these overtures than Jill Hatton, naturally a restrained actress, whose bent is now leading her to the deeper waters of legitimate theatre: she flings herself into Annie, fully determined to prove that she can sustain a long and exacting role.

Annie is a furnace quite capable of devouring every scrap of fuel that Miss Hatton can stoke into it. The remarkable fact is that at only one point, the Red Indian ritual, where the character tires but the attack must not, do the flames show signs of being allowed to die out.

Miss Hatton also realises that the part needs to be acted. (How revealing it is to hear 'You Can't Get a Man with A Gun' introduced as a plaintive song with a touch of sadness about it). Instead of the broad outline of a brash backwoods creature, she draws a softened picture of a girl conscious of her environment and needing to be reassured.

In one respect she effects a tremendous improvement in her equipment, and that is in voice production. It has to be said in the past (and with some justice) that she could not always be heard when she turned to singing. She has evidently seized upon this criticism and taken steps to rectify it; in the taxing songs of 'Annie' these efforts bring their reward, for although her delivery still lacks power the words are clear.

She has the advantage of an unselfish partner. Douglas Quarterman is a fluent actor who deals excellently with the music, and he is physically suited to the requirements of Frank Butler. Other steadying performances come from Audrey Munton, Bob Aston, and Chris Coleman. Shirley Thorne and Graham Sergent, who have a sub-plot all to themselves as a pair of young lovers, play it out with spirit. Miss Thorne's Winnie Tate is appealing, friendly, and pert.

§

Ghosts and Greasepaint

'Blithe Spirit' – Barnstaple Musical Comedy Society

One thinks of 'Blithe Spirit' as the Last Noel, the end of a chapter which established Mr Coward as the most brilliant exponent of high comedy since Oscar Wilde.

And the chapter ends there for the simple reason that his subsequent plays have not been half as sound.

To transpose Shakespeare, the good that women do lives after them; the evil's oft interred with their bones. So let it be with Elvira, lately deceased. The bereaved husband, nostalgic for her charms, has her back from the grave, remembering too late that when crossed she could prove an unmitigated shrew.

This plot, Charles Drew assembled as near a *corps d'elite* of local amateurs as we have seen for some time, players who understand very well the brittleness of style which a comedy of manners demands.

Jill Hatton, I insist, has a natural bent for this form of theatre. She made Elvira deliciously amoral, if more womanly than feline in her malice and affection, and she found something near the true spirit of Coward during the early part of the third act.

Rosemary Marsden, as the second wife, inaudible at first, was excellently controlled, although here was an unrewarding and barely sympathetic part. An overtone of sweet reasonableness was nicely disrupted here to allow the domineering personality beneath to show through.

Madame Arcati is always a potential threat to the piece; mishandled it can cause the whole atmosphere to degenerate into farce. Morag Macnab's portrayal was an exercise in brinkmanship.

Robert Aston's Charles had smugness, assurance, and wit. There were, perhaps, times when still further point could have been given to the lines. Even the support included a neat little performance by Patricia Tucker, who made the most of the maid's: 'Oh, sir' at the close.

§

Romantic lollipop for the fairer sex

'The Dancing Years' – Barnstaple Musical Comedy Society

I would say that 'The Dancing Years', which Barnstaple Musical Comedy Society present at the Queen's Hall this week, is essentially a woman's show.

By this I do not imply that men will detest it. But it has the ingredients that women are supposed to go for; tear-jerking pathos and lollipop romance.

Its hero is a broken-down and neglected composer with whom the eminently successful star of the local operetta becomes desperately enamoured.

Wanting marriage, she gets only love songs. These, however, are of so romantic a quality that they might well have been written by Ivor Novello himself.

'My dearest dear, if I could say to you in words as clear as when I play to you,' he begins. And there is a lot more in the same vein.

This is the kind of thing, I am told, that women lap up, a generalisation which was confirmed by the reaction of Monday's audience.

But there is more to Novello than sentimentality. As the piece unfolds one becomes aware of the absolute sincerity of the man and of his belief in the work as an art form.

Roy Waldron plays the part that Novello created for himself; the composer whose career is followed over the best part of two decades.

Although he copes well with the disarming arrogance and the chi-chi humour of the early passages, he hardly seems at home with the character until the passing of time has matured it.

It is the performance and personality of Dorothy Harwood, as the operetta star, which gives the play its pace and unity.

She acts with elegance and grace, although it is fair to say that she lacks some fire in her more impetuous scenes.

Her voice is powerful and pleasing and her diction is exceptionally clear. And, of course, with songs like 'Waltz of My Heart' and 'I Can Give You The Starlight' she can exercise these talents with telling effect.

Touch of restraint

Diane Bosence's technique has now improved to the point where she knows how to refrain from becoming over-strident. Her elfin dancer (the other woman in the composer's life) has freshness and a genuine girlish charm.

John Molland, on the other hand, carries restraint almost to a point of fault in his portrayal of the prince.

When the principals are off-stage, the polish fades considerably and one realises how much slack can still be taken up during the course of the run.

But Vera Ford has her moments, and when Everard Howard can act as well as he can sing, he will quickly become a force to the reckoned with.

There is plenty of colourful work for the chorus and dancers and some of the settings are lavish, but one or two of the backcloths depicting exteriors fall below the overall standard of the décor.

The producer is Arthur Garside and the musical director is Jack Thorne.

14

The Friends Dramatic Society

An event of major importance for amateur theatre in North Devon was the formation of The Friends Dramatic Society by Ann Westcott. She originally intended it as a support group for Barnstaple Grammar School where her husband, Jack, was head of history.

The company had three directors, Rosemary Marsden, a former member of the John Gay Players, Janet Potter, who had trained at the Central School of Speech and Drama, and Ann Westcott herself. The Friends shocked Devon Drama Federation by staging ten productions, all of quality, within the space of as many months.

The work was carefully divided: Ann Westcott took over the classics, Rosemary Marsden handled the lighter modern comedies, and Janet Potter took on the ultra-contemporary drama of the Theatre of the Absurd.

The schedule for one year included Arthur Miller's 'The Crucible', 'Aristophanes', 'Lysistrata', W B Yeats's 'Purgatory', Shakespeare's 'Much Ado About Nothing', Albee's 'The Zoo Story', Ionesco's 'The Lesson', Anouilh's 'Antigone', Sartre's 'In Camera', Philip King's 'See How They Run' and Pinter's 'A Night Out'.

The Friends did more than any other local amateur company to enlarge the market for classical theatre in North Devon. They also pioneered many new ventures in drama. their operations lasted through three decades. Shakespearean comedy gave several acting opportunities to Jack Westcott, whose favourite roles were probably Falstaff and Toby Belch. But one of his best performances was when he partnered Molly Hillyer in Giles Cooper's 'Everything in the Garden'. Another was with Keith Rattray, the county drama advisor for North Devon, as the two critics in Tom Stoppard's 'The Real

Inspector Hound'.

The Friends gave opportunities to several young actors who later transferred to professional theatre. Among them was Richard Quick, who played the lead in 'Charley's Aunt' and who earlier had specialised in feminine roles for Barnstaple Boys' Grammar School. He has since taken part in more than one Edinburgh Festival and has written scripts for many satirical shows for the BBC.

Another Westcott find was Ian Collier who had acted in Devon Festival Junior productions and went on to join the Shakespeare Memorial Theatre Company at the Aldwich Theatre in London. Like Quick he had been a member of the drama group at Barnstaple Boys' Grammar School.

Active members of The Friends also included Audrey Munton and June Bolam (both former members of the John Gay Players), Vera Ford, Mary Watkins and two masters from Barnstaple Grammar School, Bill Hodges and Bill Benson.

§

REVIEW 1964
(North Devon Journal)

The Cry of the Witch

Friends present Miller Play

'The Crucible' – North Devon Technical College Theatre

Arthur Miller's 'The Crucible', presented by the Friends at Barnstaple this week, blazes white hot with intolerance of intolerance.

This is an angry play, as biased in its arguments as any party-political manifesto. But the anger, like everything else about it, is expressed with a shattering economy.

And it is this economy – the taut dialogue and the lack of contrivance in construction – which makes 'The Crucible' one of our great contemporary dramatic works.

Miller, of course, has used the Salem witch trials of the 1690s, when a score of persons were hanged on the trumped-up evidence of a few teenagers, to strike a parallel with the McCarthy persecutions in America, during the 1950s.

McCarthyism is a discredited cult, at least for the moment, but the play remains a stark warning against mass-hysteria in any shape or form.

It was encouraging to find the Friends, a traditionalist society, stepping-out to attack a piece so essentially modern in idiom.

Not all that Ann Westcott attempted came off, but what did was a minor revelation, worth a baker's dozen of the sedate and static version of Shakespearean comedy which she directed last spring.

On the attack

For one thing, the acting revealed a unity so often lacking in the work of the Friends on previous occasions. The audience had cause to sense that a full-scale assault was being made on their susceptibilities and only for one short spell, in the prison scene, was the degree of tension allowed to fall slack.

The climax of the first act, when evil breaks its banks and comes pouring out in a torrent, was driven up into a crescendo of hatred, Janet Potter's Abigail, blood-curdling in its intensity of passion, being sharply defined as the immediate source of all this contagion.

The Proctors, a husband and wife whom she eventually brings down, were played with authority by Chester Lovering and Jean Morgan, the quiet dignity of the latter's portrayal forming a sounding-board for the more penetrating notes of emotion.

Sandra Squires captured the immaturity and native simplicity of Mary Warren; and William Hodges as Minister Hall; William Benson, as Minister Parris, and Jack Westcott, as Justice Danforth, added solidarity to the production.

But some of the smaller characters were also cleanly handled, notably Norman Tabberner's aged Corey and Peter Davey's court clerk.

§

REVIEW 1966
(North Devon Journal)

Non-theatre played by no-people

Becket's 'Endgame' – Beaford Arts Centre

Janet Potter, a perfectionist among local producers, finally convinced me on Friday that Samuel Beckett's 'Endgame', which she staged at Beaford Arts Centre, is a play.

Hitherto, I had accepted it as a symbolic word-pattern, depicting (as I read it) an episode near the end in the gradual running-down of the life-cycle.

Its four characters (two of them inhabit dustbins) are arguably not real people at all but rather the parts which go to make up the whole of one individual. And they are projected with deliberately shapeless plot construction in an atmosphere created to express the stifling ennui of a world which has lost faith and hope.

In other words, we have non-theatre dealing with no-people, and to build practical drama on such foundations is a task sufficient to drive any conscientious director to drink. Yet somehow Miss Potter achieved it.

Unfussed

Her attack was sharp, austere, penetrating, a simple and unfussed treatment which matched perfectly the taut quality of the language. And in Peter Davey and Patrick Cotter she found two actors of unusual sensitivity who could explore and illuminate for her the delicate relationship between the two principal figures, Clov and Hamm.

One may see Hamm (blind, bullying, crippled, and retreating from reality) as the sensual appetites, and Clov (much abused and maltreated) as the intellect. 'Endgame' hinges on the capacity of these two to communicate on a wavelength as carefully tuned as that between body and mind.

Each part was sustained on a uniform note when more variation might have deepened the dramatic cadences. A testing point was that both – and, for that matter, the limbless dustbin dwellers of Dawn Frost and Michael Hick – kept the audience thoroughly involved.

Mostly Mr Cotter did not speak his lines so much as think them, a suggestion of isolation which highlighted Hamm's dependence on his servant. Mr Davey personified the resignation of the underdog as eloquently as any OXFAM poster.

The Beaford hall, small and low-ceilinged, and jam-packed with spectators, so that some of them sat within arm's length of the cast, made its own claustrophobic contribution to this complex but deeply moving and often poetic work.

§

REVIEW 1969
(North Devon Journal)

How to get a little bit on the side

'Everything in the Garden' – The Friends

A formidable problem presented to Ann Westcott by Giles Cooper's 'Everything in the Garden' was to find two players capable of sustaining a lengthy duologue which occupies practically the whole of the first two acts.

A prodigious opening partnership is demanded, but fortunately Molly Hillyer, Hobbs to Jack Westcott's Sutcliffe in the Friends' production, has experience of the requirements of this type of innings.

Three years ago, with John Bailey, she played a Shaw two-hander for the initial season of the Beaford Centre.

And here again, at Barnstaple, on Wednesday, she was confident, poised, and polished, her brittle portrayal sharpened this time to reveal the edge so necessary in comédie noir.

Mr Westcott kept up his end of the wicket with admirable aplomb, and I would venture the suggestion that his style is better suited to modern sophisticated drama than to the robust characters in the classics, such as Falstaff and Toby Belch, with which he has become identified in the past.

Not since the well-remembered inebriation scene in 'Die Fledermaus' has he shown such lively form.

But the play was billed inappropriately by the Friends as 'delightful satirical comedy.'

Not so comic

Satire it certainly is, but I doubt whether Mr Cooper found the theme of suburban housewives adopting prostitution as a means of keeping up economically with their neighbours either delightful or comic.

His motive, it seems to me, was not to titillate or amuse, but to make a social comment on the futility and vacuousness of the prevailing materialistic way of life.

Whatever the brief given them by their publicists, the company drove home the relevance of the message.

There is savagery behind the humour in this story of money-obsessed bigots who beat their children, vote Tory, sneer at Jews and Coloureds, and despise artists as people who think they are 'different', and it was evoked, not only by the principals, but notably by Beryl Behan, William Hodges, and Suzanne Snell.

The meaty part of the Hebrew procuress was left to Audrey Munton, who attacked it with what, for her, almost amounted to self-effacement.

Such restraint deserves its reward : one cannot help speculating on what an interesting Donna Lucia she might make if Anne Westcott fulfils her threat to revive 'Charley's Aunt'.

John Colley, as the designer, had the looks and manner of the progressive, but needed a less formal style of dressing – if only to accentuate the symbolism of his murder : art crucified by an accountant's world.

§

REVIEW 1969
(North Devon Journal)

A lady who was for burning

'St Joan' – Friends Dramatic Society

The evidence of history substantiates that the individual who acts as a catalyst on his fellows tends to meet with an abrupt end.

Jesus of Nazareth was put to death on the cross; John the Baptist was beheaded; Thomas A'Becket was butchered in his own cathedral; Mahatma Gandhi and John Kennedy were shot.

Joan of Arc, the Maid of Orleans, whose visions and voices guided her to rally the French against their English oppressors was burnt at the stake.

Ann Westcott, in this Friends' production, tried to show why it had to happen.

And she found the answer in Joan's utter presumptuousness; presumptuousness towards the Church, by claiming to have her own hot-line to God; presumptuousness towards the Crown, by setting herself up as a king-maker; presumptuousness towards the Generals, by beating them at their own war-games; presumptuousness towards the Law, by making hay with its jurisprudence; and presumptuousness towards Men, by daring to become an emancipated woman in a man's world.

Country girl

The number of North Devon actresses who play in the same league as Jill Rowe may be counted on the fingers of one hand. And even among this elite corps there is none other who could have given as complete and satisfying a portrayal of Joan.

This Joan was a country girl, who combined faith, dedication, and dynamism with enormous enthusiasm for living.

The freedom that she loved was the freedom of the peasant to enjoy green fields and clean air. And this was what she wanted, for herself and for France.

She was never more convincing than at the moment when she accepted death by fire rather than renounce for ever the right to see the lark on the wing.

It was a notable performance which rightly eclipsed those around it. But the arguments in the play were carefully presented through Donald MaCallam's earthy Warwick, William Benson's persuasive De Cauchon, William Hodges's Rheims, and Jack Westcott's Lemaitre.

Howard Pierce contributed a spirited De Baudricourt, Philip Osment a vigorous and attacking De Stogumber, Paul Adams, a sincere Dunois, and Martin Wall, a peevish and introspective Charles.

The simplicity of the setting paid off handsomely, but one wondered why so much use was made of the curtain. It is also dangerous to double players like Mr MaCallam even when there are twenty parts to be filled.

§

15

Ilfracombe's Theatres

The story of Ilfracombe theatres merits a chapter in itself. At the end of the second world war there were three of them, functioning mainly, although not exclusively, during the summer months.

The Victoria Pavilion, built towards the end of the Victorian era, nestles under the shelter of Capstone and has seating capacity for around 600.

Across the main road was The Gaiety with 387 seats. The lessee was George Thomas who used the intimate and homely setting for family entertainment.

The third theatre was the Alexandra, at one time a pannier market, with seating capacity for around 700. One of its handicaps was that it was slightly removed from the seafront on one of the steepest thoroughfares in the town. I knew it particularly as the summer venue for the Rock Players who used it for seasons of rep.

The Gaiety was the first casualty, suffering a death blow through demands by Devon County Council in its safety regulations. These would have reduced seating capacity from 387 to 300, involving a possible loss of 522 patrons per week. Extra gangways, more lavatories and an additional exit were required. 'It is all too much and I cannot possibly do it', Thomas went on record as saying. 'As a company we have raised hundreds of pounds for charity and we have visited nearly every prison and asylum in the country. Now it must end.'

Hard times were also coming to the Alexandra theatre. The state of the building left quite a lot to be desired and the local council showed no great enthusiasm for footing the repairs bill.

Councillors admitted that they were ashamed of the Alexandra's condition. But in 1950 a proposal to spend all of £1,000 on improvements was rigorously slashed. 'If you continue with this squandermania there will be a robust time ahead for rate payers', one councillor warned.

By 1980 the theatre had become a local 'hot potato', following reports that it was losing £300 per week. So the building, which had been a garrison theatre throughout the war years, went dark. During the war Ilfracombe had housed a royal Army Pay Corps Office, large ATS and WRNS contingents and 'soldiers of the line', British and American, preparing for the invasion of France.

For a short while the Pavilion continued as Ilfracombe's only functioning theatre, but in the early 1980s the drama studio at Ilfracombe College began to be used increasingly for public performances. This opened a new field for amateur theatre in the town. Hitherto its amateur productions had been confined almost exclusively to light comedies and musicals, rather of the ruritanian kind. Open Theatre extended the local repertoire with such products as 'Troilus and Cressida', 'The Winter's Tale', and 'The Seagull'. It also included 'Mother Courage', Alan Bennett's 'Habeas Corpus', and the bawdy 18th century romp 'Tom Jones'.

The Victoria Pavilion meanwhile was also surviving, although somewhat precariously. During each summer it engaged resident companies to work through a season of shows, broadly in concert party style. The seasons usually opened in June and continued into September, the same show being repeated through the weeks. Then the pattern changed, with weekly visits from different companies who, from Sunday to Friday did a series of one-night stands. Top-liners who visited Ilfracombe under this system have included Frank Carson, Bernie Clifton, the Irish singer Dana, Duncan Norville, Edmund Hockridge, the Beverley Sisters and Danny La Rue.

The Pavilion's history has been fairly troubled, having suffered considerably from what might be termed 'acts of God', although it celebrate a centenary in 1987. The building was opened in a new form in 1925. Its seating capacity was 750 and the cost of modernisation was £8,000.

This structure met its end in 1949 when fire engulfed it. A London company, including Barry Lupino, were providing a summer entertainment with a show called 'Blonde in Danger'. The title may have tempted Providence. As the blaze swept through the building, the performers lost most of their possessions and the stage manager, Daphne Harvey, was lucky to escape with her life. She was changing for a swim in one of the dressing rooms when she detected smoke. She made a dash through the burning building to reach the safety of the Promenade. Station Officer Watling, of Ilfracombe Fire Service, was much praised for 'carrying on the fight gallantly' even after being struck on the head by falling tiles.

But theatre has an infinite capacity for survival. Soon rebuilding was started but only for Providence to strike again.

Another 'act of God' in the early 1990s did the Pavilion no great service. A massive storm swept over the South West and the theatre was one of its victims. Counting the cost in 1991 North Devon District Council were dismayed to find that an examination had revealed substantial structural defects. The proscenium arch had been destroyed and the balcony had suffered sufficiently to be closed until major repairs had been carried out. Estimates for remedial work ranged from £775,000 to £3,000,000, the latter figure envisaging a completely new building either at Brimlands or on the existing site.

The suggestion of a new building caught the imagination of some councillors and London architects were called in. One suggestion was that a 350-seater theatre should be provided on a new site further along the waterfront at a cost of around £1,300,000. The idea was based on the recently created Bideford College Theatre, with its 350 retractable seats. Eventually a London architect came up with what was described as 'a bold and brave proposal in contemporary style'. He envisaged the building dominated by two conical towers. This touched off the fiercest controversy that the resort had known since the demolition of the old Ilfracombe Hotel.

Opponents of the idea argued that it would be detrimental to Ilfracombe's 'Victorian image'. It was also feared that a limitation of seating to 350 would militate against the booking of nationally known 'stars'.

Champions of the scheme retaliated with the argument that the sooner Ilfracombe shed its Victorian image, the better it would be for the future of the resort.

Conservative opinion counter-attacked sharply, the proposed design being denigrated with such epithets as 'another Paddy's

Wig-wam' (a reference to Liverpool's Roman Catholic Cathedral) and, more headline making in the area's Press, 'a memorial to Madonna's bra'.

The architect himself made a trip to the town to discuss the proposal face-to-face with its detractors. Eventually a compromise is believed to have been reached, but the twin turrets seem likely at the time of writing to be retained.

16

Braunton Productions
Ilfracombe Operatic & Pantomime Societies :
The Barum & Boutport Players

B raunton Productions was formed by Rose Todd in 1974. Its first venture was a production of 'Oklahoma' directed by herself. She had an admirable male lead in Tony Evans, who combined a rugged appearance with an excellent singing voice. There was a good Laurie in Annaliese Sharp but the show-stealer, inevitably in this piece, was Cilla Harrison's Ado Annie.

It was apparent from the size of the chorus that the enterprise was not short of volunteers. Getting so large an assembly off the tiny stage of Braunton Parish Hall was a problem. A remark I made, greeted without undue local enthusiasm, was that their exits resembled a queue for the ladies' loo.

Even with musicals, the director always placed much emphasis on plot. She also chose rather off-beat shows such as 'Salad Days' and 'Little Mary Sunshine', a refreshing innovation.

She developed a 'legitimate' section. In this department she had the co-operation of a North Devon Hospital doctor, Patrick Brighten. With his wife, Mary, he had been of considerable strength to North Devon College productions. His daughter, Julie-Alanah, was a prominent member of the college group Apprentices and is now set on what promises to be a successful professional career. His introductory production was Ayckbourn's 'Season's Greetings', with Richard Haydon, Sandra Canham, Lynda McLaughlin and Nick Wood.

Braunton Productions expanded their programme further with pan-

tomimes and a junior company. They also gave summer performances at Croyde. Rose Todd's production of 'Hello Dolly' in 1984,
with its Jewish humour, carefully interpreted by Marion Scotting and
David Milner, was the most satisfying of this show that I have seen.

Eventually the group realised that Braunton Parish Hall was no
place for their activities. They transferred to the Queen's Hall in
Barnstaple where their recent productions have been held.

Except in Barnstaple and Braunton, amateur societies specialising
in musicals have had a relatively lean time during recent years.

Ilfracombe Operatic Society once had a well-established tradition,
particularly through the productions of Marie Jacobs, who continued
her efforts through a long fight against cancer. Her husband, Ted
Eley, usually took the comic leads. He had the habit of introducing
irrelevant local references to his text. Thus a Lehar operetta might be
flavoured with a comment about Capstone or Brimlands. When I
took him to task on the matter he replied 'the locals like that kind of
thing'. He believed in giving his public what they wanted, and in
other respects he was an actor of the old school.

The society's record of productions ranged from 'HMS Pinafore'
in 1946 to 'Oklahoma' in 1978. It celebrated its golden jubilee with a
'Songs from the Shows' programme in 1979, the participants including David Rigby, Eileen Candy, John Mitchell, Charles and Betty
Price, Pat Johnson and Ron Rhodes.

The society had a steady flow of talent, some of it with professional experience in former pupils of Esme Preston and other Ilfracombe
schools of dance. Among them were Anita Roberts, who had toured
the Middle East and America with her sister Penny as the Dobie
Twins (they were step-daughters of the 'North Devon Journal' sports
editor, Sydney Fyson) and Pauline Lane.

By the 1980s the society's vintage years were drawing to a close.
In spite of an heroic effort by Eileen Candy and others to save it, it
went out of existence towards the end of the decade.

Other groups have arisen to continue Ilfracombe's link with musical theatre. Ilfracombe Pantomime Society was founded in 1984 by
Pamela Beecham, a former Tiller girl and a choreographer of marked
ability, who also had a facility for writing her own locally topical
scripts.

Her first production was 'Jack and Jill' and early in 1995 she celebrated a tenth anniversary by recreating her initial show. Her husband, Geoff Beecham, one of the 1984 cast, played the dame and the good fairy was Elizabeth Kemp, with Martine Nicholls and Natalie Hughes as principal boy and girl.

Others who have worked with the group have included Ron Rhodes, Des Debelium, Dick Loxton, Pat Johnson, Pat Robinson, Paula Stairmand (sadly lost to local theatre through a fatal road accident), David Milner, Alan Bailey, Carol Pincombe and Suzanne Rudd, a highly promising youngster who determined in due course to make theatre her career.

South Molton Operatic Society are another group which have fallen by the wayside. Under the leadership of John Chilcott, they specialised in revivals of the Savoy operas and not only the better-known pieces. The Chilcott repertoire contained 'The Sorcerer', 'Ruddigore', and 'Princess Ida', with the founder-director usually taking the main roles. His collaborators included Bill Roper (then the local parson), John Bickle, Denis Cronk, Derek Stewart, Biddy Maddocks, and Henry Durston-Smith. Chilcott was 73 when, as an epilogue to these activities, he revived 'The Mikado' as a contribution to South Molton Olde English Fair.

Light opera gained a fillip in 1981 through the creation of Ilfracombe College Musical Society. Its first production was 'The Pirates of Penzance', which was followed in annual succession by 'The Gondoliers', 'The Mikado', and 'Patience'. Concern that another G & S oligarchy was developing was allayed in 1985 with 'The Merry Widow' but Gilbert and Sullivan have retained a popular place in the company's list. John Stairmand has been the group's producer. Stalwarts in his team have included Elaine Fanner, John Bradley, Dorothy Stairmand, Alastair Crighton and Val Hann.

Ilfracombe theatre has brought to the fore some accomplished singers. Among them has been Iris Casey still well remembered for the sensitivity of her treatment of 'The Sun Whose Rays'.

Barnstaple legitimate theatre has also had casualties. Notable among them was the Barum Players who began activities in the 1950s under the leadership of Kenneth James and continued until 1963. They specialised in old-time music hall but their productions included Obey's 'Noah' and Anouilh's 'Ring Round the Moon', which was chosen for a Devon drama conference presentation at

Dartington Hall. The Boutport Players, created by John Longden in 1969, had a relatively short life but it included Ionesco's 'Exit the King' with Antony Massie in the title role. Its performance at Beaford created something of a minor sensation because Jean Maudlin, portraying the soft side of the king's nature, appeared topless in one brief scene. The more realistic side was portrayed by Ann Gleave dressed in sackcloth and black leather and carrying a whip.

§

REVIEW 1969
(North Devon Journal)

Ado Annie Packs the Best Punch

'Oklahoma' – Ilfracombe Operatic Society

It might be unjust to contend that the second leads steal the show in David Rigby's production of 'Oklahoma!' for Ilfracombe Operatic Society. But they do more than anyone else to give the piece the punch that it needs.

Pauline Lane's Ado Annie is a hard-hitting performance which never loses its grip, and it is well matched in the confident handling of Will Parker by Peter Hughes.

Mr Rigby, conspicuously short of youth in his chorus, has much to thank the pair for; without their services he would have been hard-pressed to sustain anything approaching a convincing attack.

Even now, although there are no markedly slow passages, the overall pace could do with a lift.

But some of the individual performances are most competent, and the energy generated by Betty Bennington's hell-raising Aunt Ella is just the kind of storming stuff that is required.

Eileen Candy's Laurey is homely and sweet and sings nicely, which is all that can be asked of her. Alex Yates's Curly tends to be over-subdued.

Some very agreeable timing can be observed in Charles Price's Ali Hakim, who looks like Tommy Cooper and talks like Peter Sellers. John Mitchell plays Jud Fry with strong drama, creating one of the sickest and least sympathetic Juds that I have yet seen.

It was primarily the songs which made 'Oklahoma' a promoter's dream and one can never hear too much of 'The Surrey with the Fringe on Top', 'Oh What a Beautiful Morning', and 'People Will Say We're in Love'. the dream sequence is staged by Esmé Preston's dance school, with an extremely graceful Lindsay Rowe-Roberts in the principal role.

§

17

Westward Ho! Follies &
Woolacombe Repertory

A society whose efforts show little signs of flagging is Westward Ho! Follies, established by Ada Powell in 1949. In its 46-year history it has provided the resort with annual pantomimes and summer shows at the Kingsley Hall. The present company includes the children and grandchildren of some of the original cast.

I remember Mike Sale, as a lecherous sea captain in 'The Old Woman Who Lived in a Shoe', sailing his ship with the slogan 'WC' at its masthead because he was under a flag of convenience! Jackie Sharrock, in the same production played a cannibal queen.

Jacqueline Wiley grew up with the group and the musical directorship has been shared over the years between Hilda Phillips and Lionel Hodge. Another member of the company was Tim Attewell, a printer colleague at the 'Journal', who had once worked with Roy Hudd. Attewell later transferred his activities to Parkham Players who present a pantomime each year.

Westward Ho! Follies are not the only North Devon theatre company to take responsibility for entertaining summer visitors. Woolacombe Repertory have been doing so since the end of the second world war.

The group was founded by a husband-and-wife partnership Tom and Dorothy Pile. Tom had been a member of a professional group, The Wartime Players. Dorothy had also enjoye onsiderable stage experience. They came to North Devon to start a summer concert party, touring resorts on the coast.

They were joined in due course by their two daughters, Jill and Wendy, who had both trained at RADA. Other players included Ivor Gammon, whose family ran a village store at Mortehoe, David Rigby, headmaster of Woolacombe school, and Audrey Munton, a Mancunian, who had gained experience in professional repertory at Barnstaple. Others have been Joan Davies, Carole Hughes, Ray Wooff, Robin Hagley, John Bradley, Richard Haydon, Paddy Green, Margaret Molson, Brian Burch, Alan Stevens, Muriel Watts, Diane Bosence and Caroline Rowe.

The company's reputation became recognised well outside parish boundaries when it performed J B Priestley's 'When We Are Married' for a major conference at Ilfracombe. Its format is to select two plays each summer and to run them through the season, one on Tuesdays and the other on Thursdays.

Jill Rowe, who married an airline pilot and Wendy Morrall, the wife of a local hotelier, both have an aptitude for sophisticated comedy and have scored particular success with Alan Ayckbourn plots.

A performance which I remember most clearly was the virtual two-hander, 'The Rattle Of A Simple Man', which was performed, on the night I saw it, in an Ilfracombe Methodist Hall. It is the story of a Northcountry football fan 'up for the cup' in London who is having problems of a sexual nature. To try to sort out his failures with women, he visits a prostitute who also has inhibitions. It is a comedy developed with infinite sensitivity although the players (Ivor Gammon and Miss Rowe) were somewhat embarrassed by the venue chosen for it. The church congregation turned out in force to support the venture. Not many of them, I suspect, had previous knowledge of the story. My admiration was divided between the skill of the two players and the tact displayed by the local minister in proposing a vote of thanks.

§

85

Coverage in depth for Priestley

'When We Are Married' – Woolacombe and Mortehoe Players

The Church of England was once memorably described as the Conservative Party at Prayer.

By similar token it might be suggested that during the past couple of years North Devon theatre has sometimes seemed to be the Pile family at play.

Undeniably, there is talent in this clan; and rarely has it been more comprehensively or more refreshingly deployed than in J B Priestley's broad, robust, and essentially Yorkshire comedy 'When We are Married', which Jillian Rowe (a Pile in direct line of descent) produced at the Beaford Centre on Saturday as a preliminary to a five-village tour.

For my money, this is Priestley at his best. Nearly every character is a richly-drawn study of the frailty of human-nature, and Miss Rowe, apparently recruiting almost exclusively from relatives and neighbours, found a cast capable of giving coverage in depth.

Cardinal virtue

A cardinal virtue was that the flamboyant parts – Tom Pile's drunken photographer and Dorothy Pile's equally fruity charwoman – were kept, as they should be, in absolute perspective.

Attention was focused where it belonged: on the sextet of three husbands and their wives, all pillars of the local chapel, who discover during a mutual silver wedding celebration that, owing to some irregularity at their triple-marriage ceremony, they have all been 'living in sin' for twenty-five years.

In the interchanges which followed, Ivor Gammon, David Rigby, Joan Davies, Wendy Morrall, Muriel Watts and Brian Burch were able to achieve a cohesion of style which allowed the sharper edges of the humour - its good-humoured digs at Nonconformist cant and small-town pomposity - to find their mark.

Priestley wasted little time on his juvenile leads (Alan Stairmand and Susan Boyles) but his pert little 13-year-old housemaid is a minor gem of a part, and Jacqueline Ellis gave it what it was worth.

§

Nature makes strange bedmates

'Rattle of a Simple Man' Woolacombe Players

This production of Charles Dyer's sad and sensitive comedy has scarcely changed since Ivor Gammon and Jillian Rowe performed it at Ilfracombe six years ago.

That it has been preserved virtually intact is a posthumous tribute to John Longdon, the original director. Or perhaps it merely indicates the extent to which he allowed two experienced players to do it in their own way.

The story is of an encounter between social misfits, a factory worker from Manchester, whose sexual potency has been neutralised by neurotic inhibitions, and a London tart by whom, to test his abilities, he allows himself to be picked up.

The action centres on the girl's boudoir where she encourages her client to get his money's worth while he invents all manner of excuses to postpone the awful moment of going to bed.

The situation could be treated as a crude joke, but this is not Mr Dyer's intention. Instead, he examines with gentle humour and compassion the very real problems of two human beings, compelled to live in the loneliness of self-contained hells.

Fantasy world

For the prostitute also has her complexes; seduced at twelve by her step-father in the family's back-street cafe, she has escaped into her own fantasy world, inventing for herself a university education, titled connections, and ownership of the house in which she rents a sleazy flat.

In its revival, the balance of the play has moved slightly in her direction. In 1970 she was a secondary figure. Now it is she, rather than the male, who dominates the plot.

Miss Rowe has also softened her character. Its brashness is kept lurking below the surface without ever once being exposed. I believed her white lies more easily at Ilfracombe, but then, of course, I was seeing the piece for the first time.

What remains pathetically evident is her need to be wanted not for her body but for herself. And there is nothing trite about the way in which this point is made.

Mr Gammon, as always, rings true, and the courtesy and respect for women inherent in the British artisan is something which he completely understands.

Brian Burch is too chubby a brother to make this casting ideal.

18

Dulverton Players & Instow Repertory : & Other North Devon Companies

Dulverton Players are an Exmoor company which combines high level performance with a discerning choice of plays. The repertoire in recent years has included Ayckbourn's 'Relatively Speaking', Bolt's 'A Man For All Seasons', Arden's 'The Business of Good Government', Alan Bennett's 'Habeas Corpus', Rattigan's 'The Winslow Boy', Coward's 'Hay Fever', Hugh Whitmore's 'Pack of Lies', Priestley's 'When We Are Married', Shaw's Pygmalion', Frank Marcus's 'The Killing Of Sister George' and Joan Littlewood's 'Oh, What A Lovely War'. It is a repertoire of which any theatre company could be proud.

A stimulant to the group's activities has been Lionel Chilcott. He made his début with the company as a youngster and has never lost touch with it during his professional career. When on leave from his theatrical duties, he frequently returns to the Dulverton stage. He will long be remembered in the town for his performance as a paralysed sculptor in 'Whose Life Is It Anyway?', when he worked under the direction of another Dulverton stalwart, Iain Baird.

The company's stage crew usually manage to achieve miracles on the stage of Dulverton Town Hall. Another feature of their work has been their choice of introductory music. A handicap has always been the proximity to the auditorium of the refreshment bar, chattering helpers clinking cups.

Another company with an impressive record of survival is Instow Repertory, started by Brian Eratt, his first production being David Turner's 'Semi-Detached' staged in 1976.

Eratt felt that local theatre was in danger of getting too highbrow and wanted to redress the balance, or that was what he said at the time. In fact, Turner's play had a social message as an indictment of the materialism of the present age. The company included Jill Felgate, who has given the group loyal and substantial service over a couple of decades. When Coward's 'Blithe Spirit' was presented in 1979 she played Elvira to Susan Eratt's Ruth.

Soon the company decided that Instow Village Hall was no place for major productions. They moved into Barnstaple Queen's Hall where their presentations ranged from 'Shut Your Eyes And Think of England' and 'Two And Two Make Sex' to 'Ladies In Retirement' and 'Sweeney Todd'.

Richard Wheeler took over the direction from Eratt. One of his best remembered productions was 'The Wind In The Willows', undertaken with a cast numbering around 100, eighty members coming from the Slocombe-Spear School of Dance.

The close proximity of Instow Players had done nothing to inhibit Fremington's desire to have a theatre company of its own.

Master-minding the activities of Fremington Players have been another husband-and- wife partnership in Tony and Joy Blake.

They have aimed to give the parish a pantomime each year, starting the series with 'Jack And The Beanstalk' in 1984. The show was full of corny jokes – for example, 'it's cold down here so most of the cattle are friesian' – but the homely atmosphere created has been generally enjoyed.

In 1990 the company pioneered Sunday theatre, one of the first performances on the Sabbath being Derek Benfield's 'Touch And Go', a light comedy built around extra-marital sex. The company vigorously contested objections that the development would be a blow to attendance at Evensong in the local church.

HATS at Holsworthy is a North Devon stage society which owns its own 200-seater theatre. Officially, the title is Holsworthy Amateur Theatrical Society. In 1969 it opened negotiations for the purchase of the town cinema which, with the advent of television had fallen into disuse.

The move involved an amalgamation between Holsworthy Theatre Club and Holsworthy Dramatic Society. The first production of the united company was 'Relatively Speaking' directed by Bridget Pain.

Mary Kelley became the producer for Christmas pantomimes. Her

'Snow White' in 1976 drew audiences of over 3,500. Liz Squire had the title role and Philip Barfett was the ginger-wigged dame.

I describe 'Mother Goose', directed in 1985 by Annette Dennis, as the slickest of the amateur pantomimes seen in North Devon during that year. So many budding thespians were anxious to participate in 'HMS Pinafore', a venture into Savoy opera, that an augmented choir had to be accommodated in the orchestra pit.

Local drama groups, with which I have had contact, include Bishops Nympton, Molland, North Molton, Winkleigh, Hatherleigh, Bratton Fleming, Lynton (Lyn Minstrels and Lynn Dramatic Society), Croyde, South Molton (Mole Players), and Berrynarbor.

The Croyde productions were pantomimes directed by Vera Hirst. She presented them with an all-female cast because she maintained that men were less inclined to take instruction. One of her most colourful players (in name as well as in personality) was Rose Pink.

A Barnstaple company not previously mentioned is Barnstaple Rotary Amateur Theatrical Society (instigated by Denis Loosemore and called BRATS). A novel ingredient was that it had two former Chief Superintendents of Police (Reg Goldsworthy and David Morgan) in the cast.

Denis Loosemore who had played leads in musicals for Barnstaple and Ilfracombe Societies, scripted and directed Bratton Fleming pantomimes which included in its company Malcolm Prowse, leader of North Devon District council, playing the dame, and the local rector, Jonathan Richards. The musical director was Tom Courtney, a well-known local organist.

Mole Theatre's productions have included 'The Accrington Pals', a scathing commentary on the indifference to casualties displayed by Allied generals during the first world war. Courageously, they staged it during Remembrance Week.

Recent additions to the list of local drama groups have included The Renaissance Players, based on Westward Ho! and started by Ken Campbell; and a group formed by Rose Todd to support Hospice Trust.

§

REVIEW 1980
(North Devon Journal)

The mothering of lame drakes

'Candida' – Instow Repertory Company

In every clown there is said to be the desire to play Hamlet.

Similar subconscious ambitions may have prompted Instow Repertory, acknowledged champions of the theatre of escape, to perform Shaw.

Not that Shaw ever intended 'Candida' to be mistaken for what is something termed 'intellectual drama.'

Tongue-in-cheek

He clearly wrote it with tongue in cheek as a sardonic joke at the expense of contemporaries who tended to become over-earnest about romance.

It was in this spirit, I thought, that Brian Eratt approached his production.

No-one could have believed that Jill Felgate, in the title role and having to choose between husband and prospective lover, was really facing an emotional crisis of such dimensions.

It was obvious that she was bent on nothing more desperate than a self-indulgent charade, a refreshing diversion from a maternal instinct to fuss over lame drakes.

Where the portrayal scored was in its sense of period and style.

And these virtues in it found their echo in Molly Hillyer's meticulously defined Proserpine.

As for the men, what emerged from the conflict between Mr Eratt's Morell and Adrian Cole's Marchbanks was that overt masculine strength is frequently a sign of weakness.

Shaw had a sound knowledge of the way in which the male animal ticks.

Thus Morell, the formidable preacher and social reformer, a powerful Christian and a Fabian campaigner, is exposed as being more in need of womanly care and protection that the shiftless poet, a 'wretched little nervous disease,' who invades his home.

Wisely, for he is a mannered actor, Mr Eratt did not make Morell too pompous.

The strain of direction may have contributed to the fact that what registered more than the priggishness in the role was the fatigue of a public figure when his energies are almost entirely spent.

Mr Cole's Marchbanks revealed precisely enough the reserves of strength lurking beneath an exterior which was naive and insecure.

In this respect, he was typical of his calling, for poets are the modern equivalents of Old Testament prophets. And even those who are not, firmly believe themselves to be so.

Man of Business

Michael Sale did a good Burgess, the businessman who sees the world in terms of labour to be exploited and contracts to be won.

Some of the most gleefully received lines – Instow exists politically to the right of centre – were those which related to the need for the workers, and employees generally, to be kept in their place.

John Martin's industrious curate was all that a Victorian congregation would have expected him to be.

§

REVIEW 1984
(North Devon Journal)

Fate worse than death

'Whose Life Is It Anyway' – The Dulverton Players
Dulverton Town Hall

I have it on impeccable authority that, in substance and detail, Brian Clark's 'Whose Life Is It Anyway?' is a searingly accurate record of the situation it portrays.

The issue at stake involves human dignity: whether a young sculptor, permanently paralysed from the neck down through a car accident, has the right to demand to be allowed to die.

The victim has been reduced physically to the level of a vegetable. Even his bowels have to be evacuated for him.

Such humiliation he is obliged to endure with an intellect left unimpaired.

He suffers all the normal sexual urges with the knowledge that these must remain for ever unfulfilled. Every attractive nurse who ministers to him emphasises the cruelty in this aspect of his fate.

His only request of society is that the hospital support system prolonging his existence should be put to better use.

Traumatic battle

Inevitably, it is one which his doctors feel obliged to refuse. They jolly him along with bland assurances that, in due time, he will adjust and that when this happens his depression will pass.

He is too intelligent to be thus convinced, and the conflict develops into a traumatic battle of obstinate wills.

For Iain Baird's production, the role of the patient, created memorably at the Mermaid by Tom Conti, was taken by Lionel Chilcott, a former member of the Dulverton Players, who is now building a career, evidently with success, on the professional stage.

Mr Chilcott's performance was by any standards, amateur or professional, a tour de force, the finest, most moving, and most involving that I have witnessed during the past year.

It exploited to the full the acid wit which the character constantly directs against himself and his predicament.

Just as completely, it found the essential degree of charm which allows the poignancy of the humour to be pointed up.

For those who have personal acquaintance with such tragedy, it became an ordeal too painful to be missed.

Fallacy exposed

Most of all it castigated the popular fallacy that bodily affliction necessarily goes hand-in -hand with affliction of the mind.

It is the 'does he take sugar in his tea?' kind of patronage that the occupant of the wheelchair will always find hardest to bear.

The supporting company played up well to maintain a level in the acting. Major contributions included Pam Poat's as the ward sister, Keith Ross's as the male orderly, Ingrid Slater's, as the junior registrar, Iain Baird's, as the consultant physician, and David Stodd's as the judge.

Mr Baird's was a skilfully sympathetic treatment of what, in the context of the plot, had to be a basically unsympathetic role.

There was good work also from Philip Jones, as the artist's solicitor, and Jane Heath, as the barrister who brings a writ of habeas corpus to court.

Helen Jones, Evelyn Cornell, Graham Poat, Mike Littlewood, and Ros Pope had the smaller parts, and Alan Hearth designed a splendidly sectionalised set.

§

19

From Dance to Youth Theatre :
Ilfracombe's Channel Festival

To do them credit, local dance schools have done much to introduce the youth of the area to theatre. A youth event which is establishing its place in the more serious aspects of the North Devon drama calendar is the Channel Festival, held during the high summer at Ilfracombe.

It was created in 1986, primarily through the efforts of Liz Baines and Jon Bell. Bell, outlining its aims in 1987, said that it offered young people the chance to perform for others, to demonstrate different media, and to swop ideas.

Contributions were presented in a variety of locations, from church halls to marquees on the seafront. Some were performed in the open-air on Wildersmouth Beach.

By 1988 the festival had doubled its original size with forty groups participating. They included a Norwegian brass band. Professional support came from television's Friday Night Live comic mime artist, Less Bubb, and Zootes and Spangles, a black American jazz dance group.

The Orchard's youth theatre, which Andrew Mulligan established and later became known as Unit 108, was one of the initial supporters and there was also backing from Ilfracombe College. The college had contributed a full length 'As You Like It'. One innovation was provided by the Dayspring Sacred Dance Group who demonstrated how theatre could be incorporated into worship. Ben Baddoo gave an exhibition of African drumming and dance. Ad Hoc Stage Company explored the relationship between Charles Chaplin and Stan Laurel.

Devon Youth theatre dramatised the life of the English radical, Tom Paine. Two of the participants, Sasha Keegan and Samantha Hughes, of Solihull Youth Theatre, liked Ilfracombe so much that they decided to stay.

In 1989 British Telecom stepped in with an offer of £50,000 to enable a former Telecom station at Mullacott Cross to become a centre for young musicians and to serve as a base for festival operations. There was also a £25,000 contribution from the Government's business sponsorship scheme.

The 1989 festival survived heavy rain, thunder, and lightning. There were other setbacks. A tent peg, being hammered in to support a marquee, severed an electricity cable and succeeded in blacking out the whole of the seafront.

I reviewed two of the productions, by Youth Action Theatre and Central Youth Theatre. Youth Action had come only as observers but were so impressed that they decided to participate. They evolved a piece about two odious children who got their kicks by playing practical jokes and whose activities eventually precipitated nuclear war.

Central Youth Theatre's 'The Day Truth Broke Out' earned the reputation of being the festival's X certificate show. This was because of a scene which simulated mass copulation, innocuous enough in its context but, as I commented at the time, likely to cause misapprehensions when rehearsed in public in the open air.

Other contributions, including Solihull Youth Theatre's 'Watch This Space' and Youth Studio Theatre's 'Daisy Pulls It Off' were reviewed by a young colleague who had co-produced for the local Studio Theatre, Katie Jones. She complained vigorously about chattering audiences and backstage noise, vices only too prevalent in many adult shows.

By 1990 the festival had received national recognition and had drawn Arts Council interest. In 1992, Trestle Theatre's 'Hanging Around' drew capacity audience at the Victoria Pavilion and intending patrons had to be turned away.

Penny Jackson, wife of the head of drama at Ilfracombe College, had become festival administrator. By 1992 the number of participants had increased to well over 500. An innovation in 1993 was a visit from the Lithuanian Academy of Music and Drama, who joined the Orchard's 108 youth unit in Dante's 'Inferno'. It was an exchange visit between the groups which had been given a place at a Royal National Theatre festival and was believed to be the first British-Lithuanian cultural exchange.

Imago, from North Devon College, staged Pinter's 'The Dumb Waiter' and entries came from as far afield as Newcastle and Southampton. Other contributors included Manchester's Lesbian and Gay Youth.

20

The Church & Its Theatrical Spin-Off

The Church has played a distinguished part in the development of North Devon theatre. The involvement of its clergy probably began with Prebendary Edmund Boggis, when he was vicar of the now demolished St Mary Magdalene's Church in Barnstaple. In the January of 1914 he assembled a cast of about 200 to present a pageant of the history of Barnstaple, the scenes including the preaching of St Brannock, King Athelstan founding Barnstaple Fair, Sir Richard Grenville enlisting recruits to fight against the Spanish Armada and the sojourn in Barnstaple, during the Civil War (at the residence of a Mistress Beaple in Southgate Street, now the southern end of High Street) of the heir to the throne later to become King Charles the Second. The pageant, presented at the Theatre Royal, received much publicity in the national press.

In more recent times, Prebendary Arthur Chandler, vicar of Ilfracombe, who played Becket in a Festival of Britain performance of 'Murder in the Cathedral' at Barnstaple, was also a founder member of Argosy Players, started in 1952 by the then county drama adviser for North Devon, Stella Farrow. It was a travelling theatre group, other members including Arthur Filsell, who had produced plays for Barnstaple Girls' Grammar School and had acted in Lynton productions, Peter Ramsden, Richard Falkner, Quenten Morris, Neil Adams, Alfred Baskerville, Jack and Vera Willett, Lilian Goodspeed, Jeanette Chandler, Patrick Warrington, Rosemary Bailey, Hilda Gosman, and Hugh Brooks. there were no less than three parsons in the team, which made a debut with 'Tobias And The Angel', produced by Joan Lennard of Chittlehampton Manor.

Arthur Chandler was the North Devon chaplain of the Actors'

Church Union and each year, usually towards the end of the summer season, he held an actors' service in Ilfracombe Parish Church. The cast of Ilfracombe's resident seasonal shows, as well as local amateurs, took part. It was a concept that ceased to be fully effective when the seasonal entertainment developed into one-night stands.

Quenten Morris was the incumbent at Bishops Nympton, and was in at the early stages of the activities of Bishops Nympton Players who celebrated their silver jubilee in 1992. Their record has centred mainly on light comedies although they occasionally extend their repertoire to include such plays as 'Lord Arthur Saville's Crime'.

Prebendary Roger Reeve, now vicar of Braunton, started the St Peter's Players when he was a curate in Barnstaple during the 1960s. Prebendary H L Franklyn was a founder of the Newport Players at Barnstaple. Bratton Fleming Drama Group has had sustained assistance from the local rector, Jonathan Richards and, also previously mentioned, Prebendary Bill Roper has played leads for South Molton Operatic Society. John Marks, head of drama at the North Devon College is also a priest in the Orthodox Church.

Churches have frequently been used to stage drama. St Peter's at Ilfracombe is admirably suited to open-stage productions. Barnstaple Parish Church has had a number of plays performed on the steps of its chancel. In addition to 'Murder In The Cathedral' these have included the first performance in North Devon of the morality play 'The Castle Of Perseverance', presented by a company of Oxford and Cambridge students at the instigation of Prebendary Tom Owen, then vicar of Holy Trinity, Barnstaple. The church has also been used by Orchard Theatre for a revival of the old Yorkshire Mysteries and for a play built around the somewhat eccentric career of Parson Hawker, of Morwenstowe, who ran a one-man campaign against wrecking, at that time a major industry on the local coast.

At Bideford Parish Church in the early 1950s Elizabeth Stucley presented her own biblical drama 'The Promised Land', a saga tracing the story of the Hebrew race from its creation to the time of Christ. Arthur Chandler played Noah in 'The Flood' and Moses in 'The Exodus', two of the episodes in the Stucley play.

Another play on a religious theme was 'Pontius Pilate', performed at Braunton by the Mystery Players and produced by William Atkins. The author was the local Congregational minister, the Reverend J

Welham Clarke.

Drama continued to play its part in the activities of Bideford Parish Church, where Vera Gilson introduced the St Mary's Players. Later the daughter church at East-The-Water had its own drama group, a leading member of which was Richard Baron.

One of the most emotionally moving plays that I have witnessed in a church setting was Ronald Duncan's treatment of the Abelard and Heloise story, directed by the author in the magnificent Stoke Church at Hartland. Staged in 1970 it had as its two principals two talented professionals, Denis Goacher and Antoinette Moat. Abelard was a lecturer in 11th century Paris. Heloise was the niece of a canon of Notre Dame Cathedral. They fell in love and consummated their passion, with the result that as a punishment Abelard was castrated and the heartbroken Heloise retired to a convent. They continued to communicate by letter, producing in the process some of the finest literature of all time. Antoinette Moat gave her performance at a writing desk in the nave. Goacher, similarly seated, was positioned aloft on the rood screen. the illusion of both nearness and distance, as lights switched from one character to the other, was poignantly conveyed.

Tradishaw Players, which flourished from the 1960s to the early 1980s took its title from the names of three villages on the road from Barnstaple to Torrington. They were Horwood, Alverdiscott, and Newton Tracey, and they formed the initial base of the group's operations.

The local rector, Bernard Tinsley, and his wife, Eileen, were prominent members. Others on the playing strength included doctors and teachers.

If I remember correctly there was some disagreement over company policy. One faction felt that the object should be to provide entertainment for the three villages and that plays should be chosen accordingly: nothing of a BBC Third Programme nature. Others argued with some justification that there was sufficient talent on hand to be more ambitious, to go further afield with material of higher quality. The argument was conducted in a very civilised manner, and I wished one or two of the other North Devon societies would follow the example. Some annual meetings that I have attended have deteriorated into virtual slanging matches.

A member of Tradishaw was Guy Pertwee, a retired captain of the

Royal Navy and a local councillor. He was a staunch patriot and a true-blue Tory. Often he would chide me, in friendly fashion, for giving 'undue publicity' to plays which he felt had a Left Wing bias. I suspect that he regarded most modern dramatists as being Red propagandists.

Three generations of his family were represented in the group. It included his daughter, Geraldine Crowther, and her daughter, Susan who made her début in a Stan Forrester production of Norman Holland's 'Judgement Here'.

The company had a liking for Aldwych farces, such as 'Thark', 'Rookery Nook', and 'Tons of Money'. Molly Hillyer, a teacher at Bideford School, directed Shaw's 'Arms and The Man'. The Riana was Louise Macmillan and Louka was Dinah Clark.

Torrington Museum Project sponsored Noel Coward's 'Relative Values'. Three doctors, David Gibson, Jeremy Bartlett and Julian Turner were involved. In Gordon Daviot's 'Remember Caesar', set in restoration England, Bob and Barbara Terrell had the support of a young Bideford actor who subsequently became a professional, Cyril Squires.

Perhaps Tradishaw's most memorable achievement was the commemoration of Thomas Becket's assassination (29th December, 1170) on the precise day of the 800th anniversary of the murder. The prologue was given by Geraldine Crowther, a direct descendant of William de Traci, one of the assassins. After the crime, de Traci flew to his family seat in North Devon where he built the church at Newton Tracey in which the performance was given. He also built a chapel at the end of Barnstaple Long Bridge dedicating both of them to Becket as atonement for the sin. The play, needless to say, was Eliot's 'Murder In The Cathedral' produced by Stan Forrester with Dick Baylis, at the time headmaster of Chittlehampton School, in the Becket role.

When one village group ceases activities another invariably rises. In this case it was Nomads, the dramatic society of North Molton. The first I saw of them was in 1984 when they staged Gerald Savory's 'A Month of Sundays'. The director was Betty Kirk.

In 1989 she handled an unabridged version of Oscar Wilde's 'The Importance of Being Earnest'. A recruit from Dulverton Players, John Fulford-Williams, commented: 'She's the boss and what she says goes'. In 1988 North Molton staged a pantomime, 'The Sleeping Beauty' but this was not officially a Nomads' venture. It was performed by an all-male cast called the Gentlemen of All Saints. The local parson, Gilbert Cowdry, had the title role.

Drama groups linked to ecclesiastical foundations might reasonably expect that Providence would protect them from unwarranted misfortunes. This has not always been the case.

St Paul's Players, with attachment to the Barnstaple Anglican Church at Sticklepath, had a traumatic experience when they staged a production in the church hall. Half way through the performance the actors were disconcerted to see their set disintegrating around their ears. The result could hardly have been more traumatic if it had been hit by a scale 10 earthquake. An elaborately prepared fireplace collapsed into rubble with the dignity of a high-rise office block suffering a controlled demolition by Blaster Bates.

§

REVIEW 1970
(North Devon Journal)

Tragedy of star-crossed lovers

'Abelard and Heloise' – Stoke Church, Hartland

Christians live in the faith that God is love. Ronald Duncan, a Christian poet among a generation of unbelievers, has always seemed to accept as his creed that love is God.

Time and again in his writing we find love exalted as the supreme and most ennobling emotion, embracing all that is highest and best and most worthwhile in man.

In 'Don Juan' it is love, a love which transcends death, that redeems evils; in 'Judas' it is love, and not avarice, which brings the disciple to betray his Christ.

For 'Abelard and Heloise' which he directed personally at Hartland this week, Mr Duncan turns for his theme to one of the greatest and most tragic love-stories of all time.

Abelard was a lecturer in 11th century Paris; Heloise, the niece of a canon of Notre Dame Cathedral. They fell in love and consummated their passion, but the enraged uncle drove them apart.

Abelard was castrated and sent to a monastery. The heartbroken Heloise retired to a convent. But they continued to write each other letters. And it is these letters which form the substance of Mr Duncan's play.

Nave-to-gallery

The setting in the magnificent church building at Stoke gave dramatic impact to the performance. Antoinette Moat as Heloise, was seated, in her nun's habit, at a writing desk in the nave. The Abelard, Denis Goacher, similarly seated, was positioned aloft on the gallery of the rood-screen.

Lights switched from one to the other as, thinking aloud, they committed their emotions to paper. The point was poignantly made that, while minds were communicating, physical contact was denied.

At the London production, about ten years ago, a general criticism was that the intonation of monologues was too static an exercise to keep an audience involved for the best part of two hours.

Yet lack of action was scarcely apparent here. Miss Moat could bring a wealth of movement into a gesture of the hand, and Mr Goacher could do as much with vocal inflection.

And the words themselves took on such rhythmic patterns that there was a temptation to hear them with the eyes shut so that no disturbing visual factor might intrude.

The text was well served by the actors. Mr Goacher has a resonant delivery and a quality of diction encountered all too infrequently in the theatre these days. Miss Moat burned with the anguish of a woman torn from heaven to suffer in hell.

'I love you wholly,' writes Heloise, ' and behind that word is my hand, and behind that hand is my blood.'

The total commitment and soul-searing intensity of this love glowed white-hot in Miss Moat's portrayal.

It is in such love, Mr Duncan seems to me to suggest, that man will find God.

§

21

The New Queen's Theatre

B y the 1990s North Devon District Council seemed to be developing a deeper interest in theatre. One reason may have been the appointment of an arts officer, Rosemarie Pitts (Lyons).

While there was no dissatisfaction with the Queen's Hall programme there was a widespread criticism of the building itself. Many said that it resembled a warehouse rather than a theatre. By 1993 the council had decided to do something about it.

They called in Alex Medhurst, who was born in Toronto and had renovated four arts centres in Canada.

By the May of 1993 a fund-raising drive had achieved support from local businesses large and small. A sum of almost £900,000 was in the bank, of which the council had provided £750,000 and £100,000 had been added by the Foundation for Sport and Arts. Barnstaple Town Council found £30,000 and South West Water contributed £5,000.

The cost of the conversion had been put at £1,200,000 and Medhurst was able to forecast that Barnstaple would soon possess 'a theatre for the next century'. Administrative control was also changed, passing from the council itself to a board of trustees, the chairman being Bob Beattie, senior partner of a North Devon firm of solicitors.

Alex Medhurst did not remain in North Devon to see the completion of the restoration. Later in 1993 he was appointed to direct a £2,500,000 conversion of a customs house in Newcastle into two theatres and an art gallery.

By the end of the year the old Queen's Hall was ready to blossom as the Queen's Theatre, under the management of Rick Bond, whose tenure of office as director of the Beaford Centre had been followed by a highly successful managership of the Taunton Brewhouse Theatre.

A major improvement from the public's point of view was the provision of raked seating in the stalls. It meant that at last anyone occupying a seat would have an uninterrupted view of the stage.

The changes in the structure of the building have been internal rather than external. The frontages designed by Gould nearly a century-and-a-half ago have been preserved as a link with Barnstaple's cultural past.

The foyer has been embellished with a modern computerised box-office and a bar. There has been an improvement in acoustics through the installation of baffles and the old central heating plant has been replaced. New flooring in the stalls matches other woodwork in American cherry. The background colouring for walls and carpets is a deep midnight blue.

The new theatre could scarcely have had a better opening show than Mark Cartier's pantomime 'Snow White'. I was in New Zealand when the run opened but Kate Helyer, reviewing for the 'Journal', avowed that everything about the occasion was 'polished and pristine'.

The first Rick Bond season provided the public with the kind of theatre expected to be found in London. An early and memorable event was a production by Talawa Theatre of 'King Lear' with a predominantly coloured cast. Some people anticipated that it would be incongruous to see a tragedy of ancient Britain performed by coloured actors. In fact this inconsistency was not even noticed. Ben Thomas's Lear was physically lithe and not particularly senile. He eschewed the traditional long white beard in favour of a more austere and closer cut. But from his first appearance sheer madness glistened fiercely in his eyes. There was a fine Edmund from David Harewood, and Mona Hammond made an engagingly comic fool.

Mid-Wales Touring Theatre presented an adaptation by Mike Jones (presumably no relation) of Henry Fielding's 'Tom Jones'. The original story, written in the late 1740s, is by modern standards, verbose. Mike Jones compressed it, without loss of fluency, into a play lasting for a mere two and a half hours.

Paul Barnhill made Tom not so much a lecher as a young man anxious to explore his sexuality. Sarah-Louise Mayne's Sophie was obviously intrigued by his personality in the way that well-brought-up girls tend to be attracted to males of dubious reputation. Louise Richard's Molly was a harlot who believed that Tom was the answer to her unmaidenly prayers.

The Rick Bond technique was broadly based to cover a wide range of tastes. Another booking was Brian Rix and his wife, Elspet Gray, in what amounted to an unashamed plug for Rix's latest book 'Tour de Farce'.

With Terence Frisby's 'Rough Justice' Barnstaple had a taste of a play booked for London. Robert Herford's production had Martin Shaw and Diana Quick in the key roles. Shaw played a media personality accused of murdering his handicapped baby son. Miss Quick played the prosecuting attorney and Alan Dobie the judge.

Su Pollard played the lead in 'Little Shop of Horrors' and a highly sophisticated programme was presented by Fascinating Aida.

Variations were provided by Natural Theatre's 'Henry The Eighth, A Serial Killer' and English touring Theatre presented 'As You Like It'.

The North Devon Public have thus experienced a variety of quality events.

Two outstanding bookings, in addition to King Lear, have been Travelling Opera's 'La Traviata' and Shared Experience's adaptation by Helen Edmundson of George Eliot's 'The Mill On the Floss', as emotionally involving as any play seen in North Devon for several years.

The theatre has not been without its critics. Local amateur companies have found that hiring costs for their productions have risen somewhat spectacularly and some have found alternative venues. Others are hoping that the trustees will offer them special consideration.

§

Mad, Sad, and a very good show

'King Lear' – Talawa Theatre Company, Queen's Theatre

Talawa is an ethnic drama company formed eight years ago. Its contribu
tion to the Queen's Theatre gala season was a 'King Lear' with a predominantly coloured cast.

A virtue of Shakespeare's tragedies is their universality. They deal with
problems which, throughout history, have bedevilled people of all races,
classes, and creeds.

'Macbeth' is a warning against ambition, 'Othello' against jealousy, and
'Coriolanus' against the power complex. 'Romeo and Juliet' is a condemna-
tion of gang warfare, and so on.

What is examined in 'King Lear' is the perplexities of a mind distorted
by old age. The play also explores the ruthless impatience of heirs-appar-
ent to achieve the inheritance which they feel is long overdue.

Not that Ben Thomas's Lear was particularly senile. Physically he was
lithe, and like Cassius he had a lean and hungry look. He eschewed the
traditional long white beard in favour of a more austere and closer cut.

But from his first appearance sheer madness glistened fiercely in his
eyes.

He craved the flattery of two of his daughters, Lolita Chakrabarti's
Goneril and Cathy Tyson's Regan. When he got none of it from Diane
Parish's spirited Cordelia he banished her from his sight.

For years Lear was considered virtually unactable. Thespians of the
Victorian and Edwardian eras shunned it like the plague. More recently
players of the calibre of Olivier, Gielgud, and Scofield have made nonsense
of such contentions and a steady stream of performers have followed in
their wake.

The Thomas Lear was too bitter to provoke instant sympathy. Its full
pathos was not felt until the final scene, when he carried in the body of
the murdered Cordelia. 'I killed the slave that was a hanging thee' was
uttered with a desperate note of remorse.

Yvonne Brewster's productions was full of splendid effects. The storm
was the most vivid that I have seen, the building shaking to the thunder.
The battle scene, with troops bearing riot-shields was another spectacular
success.

There was a fine Edmund from David Harewood, whose delivery testi-
fied to his training at RADA and Mona Hammond made an engagingly
comic fool, although elsewhere the lighter moments did not always come
off.

§

REVIEW 1995
(North Devon Journal)

'The Mill on the Floss'

Shared Experience – Queen's Theatre

The Queen's Theatre has again become the first port of call in an international tour.

Helen Edmundson's adaptation of George Eliot's 'The Mill on the Floss', presented by Shared Experience, is scheduled to visit Germany, India, Sri Lanka, and Bangladesh.

It proved to be as spectacularly dramatic and as emotionally involving as any play seen in North Devon during the past twelve months.

George Eliot, of course, was a woman who wrote under a male pseudonym to shield her activities from the chauvinistic prejudices of the Victorian era.

Her heroine in the story, Maggie Tulliver, probably reflected her own temperament and the social complexities thus involved.

Maggie was portrayed in turn by three actresses. Anne-Marie Duff was the youthful Maggie, wild, rebellious, energetic and intellectual. Catherine Cussack was Maggie Mark II, resigned to a compromise with accepted standards and casting aside artistic leanings. The third Maggie was Helen Schlesinger, revealing the result of all these experiences as, haunted by the ghosts of earlier phases in her development, she tries to come to terms with her life.

The men in her life were played by Simon Cox, as Maggie's brother, the son of a bankrupt miller and anxious to restore the family fortunes, requiring her to assist him by respecting conventions, Michael Matus, physically handicapped but conscious of her artistic needs, and Jonathan Cake, a romantic who falls for her feminine charm.

The play has a strong element of symbolism, particularly as one Maggie is translated, looking into a mirror, into the next. The opening with a ducking of a suspected witch was traumatic. The action was full of movement and the finale, involving a flood, must have been given topical relevance by recent happenings in Japan.

§

22

Exit

I am aware that my half-century as a theatre critic has given me opportunities to do precisely what I hoped to do when I came into journalism. My ambition to write for newspapers started at the age of six. It horrified my mother, who regarded such unorthodox professions as being almost anti-social.

When I went for an interview with the headmistress of my preparatory school, the first question that she asked me was what I wanted to be when I grew up. No doubt she expected me to say that I had ambitions to drive racing cars or railway locomotives. Instead I replied that I wanted to 'write for the newspapers'. Even I was aware that her jaw dropped.

Needless to say it has given me great pleasure to be able to remain in North Devon, still one of the finest parts of the country, and to witness the cultural expansion which has occurred since the end of the war.

I am completely out of sympathy with the large number of local residents who still say that the area is a cultural desert when I know from experience that it is nothing of the kind. I would like them to have sight of my theatre diary for one of the recent years. They would be astonished at the number of entries that each month contains.

Of course, I realise that very substantially theatre has become a spectator rather than a participatory activity. Professional companies are now providing the lion's share of performances but I firmly believe that the ultimate result of this development will be that standards of discernment will rise.

REVIEW 1978

(North Devon Journal)

Sir Toby with a slimline image

'Twelfth Night' – The Royal Shakespeare Company

Not all that often does the Royal Shakespeare Company take to the road.

The 'Twelfth Night' which it brought to the Plough this week has pleased the critics.

More significantly perhaps, it has drawn capacity houses at each stop on its provincial tour.

And deservedly so, for John Amiel's platform production is swift, intimate, and inventive.

One of its surprises is that this most Elizabethan of comedies has been taken out of its period and performed in Edwardian dress.

Another is Ian McKellen's Toby, no longer a fat knight but a dapper country squire, sprightly and brimming with fierce enthusiasm for life.

This Toby is a man of breeding, with a public school background. The sheer glee in him has occasional touches which are Chaplinesque.

Contempt

His contempt for Malvolio is complete, and firmly founded on a general antipathy towards bigots and social-climbers, an attitude very evident in rural England half-a-century or so ago.

It is around Toby's scenes that the action really revolves, and he is well served by the Aguecheek of Roger Rees, who accepts with philosophical good-humour the fact that he was born to be an ass.

Bob Peck's Malvolio combines the appearance of Alfred Marks with the accent of Wilfred Pickles. His cross-gartered posturing becomes, at least to Southerners, as outrageous a piece of North-country-effrontery as Arthur Scargill's latest wage demands.

Bridget Turner's Maria, although sharp, is relatively subdued, but Christopher Hancock's Feste, a comic well past his prime, retains the attribute of a dry and wise wit.

The romantic plot has a wistful Viola by Emily Richard and Edward Petherbridge as a silvering Orsino, besotted to an extent which, I am told, can occur only when a man is over the forty-mark.

Suzanne Bertish's Olivia is gentle with Feste, impatient with unrequited suitors, and eager to a point of abandon when she sees what she wants. Of all the characters, she is the most Edwardian in style.

§

Fast lane for Slowe

Romeo and Juliet – Royal Shakespeare Company

The visit of the Royal Shakespeare Company to Barnstaple this week has been publicised as a celebration of the Link Road.

The play selected is Romeo and Juliet: some might consider 'The Comedy of Errors' to have been a more appropriate choice.

But Terry Hands offers a fast-lane production. The sword fighting for instance, looks as though it is for real.

One could hardly expect more determined violence, except possibly on the terraces during the World Cup.

Notwithstanding the fact that the stage is an overcrowded profession, I am happy to state that most of the players seem to have survived a nine-week tour. Providence and Equity have obviously done a deal.

The tempo throughout is highly athletic which may justify the choice of the North Devon Leisure Centre as a venue. The cut-and-thrust makes nonsense of the fallacy, encouraged by generations of bad teaching, that Shakespeare is necessarily dull.

Since Zeffirelli, the public have come to expect visual stimulation to supplement the plot. Performance in the arena and on a bare stage still allows, through masque and music, for the creation of a magnificently Renaissance mood.

One critic described the love scenes as 'like gunpowder explosions.' They steam with passion, with Georgia Slowe's Juliet thoroughly convincing as a 14 year old desperately eager to consummate newly-discovered desires.

This sparkling-eyed Juliet is the most captivating that I have seen since Claire Bloom's.

Mark Rylance sees Romeo legitimately as adolescent, slightly winge-ing and basically immature.

Vincent Regan's Tybalt breathes hate and aggression. There is a dry humour in David O'Hara's Mercutio, sometimes ebullient and occasionally moody, and Janet Heslewood is a caring nurse.

One appreciates particularly the Benvolio of Patrick Brennan, the heavy-father in the Capulet of Bernard Horsfall and the honesty of Patrick Godfrey's Friar Laurence. But without doubt this is Miss Slowe's play.

§

Devil of a monarch

King Richard III – Royal Shakespeare Company

Continuing a crusade to bring quality drama to the remote regions, the Royal Shakespeare Company is presenting King Richard III at the North Devon Leisure Centre this week.

The title role is taken by the up-and-coming Simon Russell Beale. His Richard is a study in sheer ruthless amorality. His delivery has a ring of steel which develops, when he is frustrated, into a plaintive whine.

Like Olivier's film creation there is an element of tongue-in-cheek camp in it. This is a fine companion-piece for Sir Ian McKellen's modern-dress rendering - a military martinet with clipped Sandhurst-style speech - which I saw at the National earlier this year.

Beale is his own man, weaving a pattern well removed from McKellen's. Bald, malformed, loping and physically repulsive, he is evil incarnate, stabbing colleagues in the back and leering his way through the seduction of any female – like Annabelle Apison's Lady Anne – who can help him to further his own ends.

Historians will tell you that as faction (fiction posing as fact) the play leaves several television series as limp also-rans.

Obviously, it went down well with the Tudors, thus guaranteeing the author subsidised support.

The devilry in this Richard is somewhat redeemed by a sharp wit, and Beale even provokes sympathy in the run-up to Bosworth Field.

Curses

Sam Mendes' chilling and economic production is strong at all levels, and notably so in Stephen Boxer's Buckingham and Cherry Morris' queen Margaret, reiterating curses at every opportunity.

The costuming is modernistic, with sufficient traditional overtones to make relevant such desperate appeals as, 'my kingdom for a horse'.

§